Visual FoxPro Certification Exams Study Guide

Cindy Winegarden
Evan Delay

Hentzenwerke Publishing

Published by:
Hentzenwerke Publishing
980 East Circle Drive
Whitefish Bay WI 53217 USA

Hentzenwerke Publishing books are available through booksellers and directly from the
publisher. Contact Hentzenwerke Publishing at:
414.332.9876
414.332.9463 (fax)
www.hentzenwerke.com
books@hentzenwerke.com

Visual FoxPro Certification Exams Study Guide
    By Cindy Winegarden and Evan Delay
    Technical Editor: Tamar E. Granor
    Copy Editor: Farion Grove

ISBN: 1-930919-04-2

Manufactured in the United States of America.

To Daddy:
"There *IS* a light at the end of the tunnel."

—Cindy Winegarden

I would like to dedicate this book to my wife, Kimberly.

—Evan Delay

Our Contract with You, The Reader

In which we, the folks who make up Hentzenwerke Publishing, describe what you, the reader, can expect from this book and from us.

Hi there!

I've been writing professionally (in other words, eventually getting a paycheck for my scribbles) since 1974, and writing about software development since 1992. As an author, I've worked with a half-dozen different publishers and corresponded with thousands of readers over the years. As a software developer and all-around geek, I've also acquired a library of more than 100 computer and software-related books.

Thus, when I donned the publisher's cap four years ago to produce the *1997 Developer's Guide,* I had some pretty good ideas of what I liked (and didn't like) from publishers, what readers liked and didn't like, and what I, as a reader, liked and didn't like.

Now, with our new titles for 2000, we're entering our third season. (For those who are keeping track, the '97 DevGuide was our first, albeit abbreviated, season, and the batch of six "Essentials" for Visual FoxPro 6.0 in 1999 was our second.)

John Wooden, the famed UCLA basketball coach, had posited that teams aren't consistent; they're always getting better—or worse. We'd like to get better…

One of my goals for this season is to build a closer relationship with you, the reader. In order for us to do this, you've got to know what you should expect from us.

- You have the right to expect that your order will be processed quickly and correctly, and that your book will be delivered to you in new condition.

- You have the right to expect that the content of your book is technically accurate and up-to-date, that the explanations are clear, and that the layout is easy to read and follow without a lot of fluff or nonsense.

- You have the right to expect access to source code, errata, FAQs, and other information that's relevant to the book via our Web site.

- You have the right to expect an electronic version of your printed book (in compiled HTML Help format) to be available via our Web site.

- You have the right to expect that, if you report errors to us, your report will be responded to promptly, and that the appropriate notice will be included in the errata and/or FAQs for the book.

Naturally, there are some limits that we bump up against. There are humans involved, and they make mistakes. A book of 500 pages contains, on average, 150,000 words and several megabytes of source code. It's not possible to edit and re-edit multiple times to catch every last misspelling and typo, nor is it possible to test the source code on every permutation of development environment and operating system—and still price the book affordably.

Once printed, bindings break, ink gets smeared, signatures get missed during binding. On the delivery side, Web sites go down, packages get lost in the mail.

Nonetheless, we'll make our best effort to correct these problems—once you let us know about them.

In return, when you have a question or run into a problem, we ask that you first consult the errata and/or FAQs for your book on our Web site. If you don't find the answer there, please e-mail us at **books@hentzenwerke.com** with as much information and detail as possible, including 1) the steps to reproduce the problem, 2) what happened, and 3) what you expected to happen, together with 4) any other relevant information.

I'd like to stress that we need you to communicate questions and problems clearly. For example…

- "Your downloads don't work" isn't enough information for us to help you. "I get a 404 error when I click on the **Download Source Code** link on **www.hentzenwerke.com/book/downloads.html**" is something we can help you with.

- "The code in Chapter 10 caused an error" again isn't enough information. "I performed the following steps to run the source code program DisplayTest.PRG in Chapter 10, and I received an error that said 'Variable m.liCounter not found'" is something we can help you with.

We'll do our best to get back to you within a couple of days, either with an answer or at least an acknowledgment that we've received your inquiry and that we're working on it.

On behalf of the authors, technical editors, copy editors, layout artists, graphical artists, indexers, and all the other folks who have worked to put this book in your hands, I'd like to thank you for purchasing this book, and I hope that it will prove to be a valuable addition to your technical library. Please let us know what you think about this book—we're looking forward to hearing from you.

As Groucho Marx once observed, "Outside of a dog, a book is a man's best friend. Inside of a dog, it's too dark to read."

Whil Hentzen
Hentzenwerke Publishing
April 2001

List of Chapters

Table of Contents

Chapter 2: Developing a Logical Data Model   17

Chapter 3: Deriving the Physical Design   29

Chapter 10: Deploying an Application   145

Chapter 11: Maintaining and Supporting an Application   155

Foreword

When I learned that the *Visual FoxPro Certification Exams Study Guide* was in the works, I was ecstatic. Not only because you, reader, are going to be learning from very respected Visual FoxPro developers like Cindy Winegarden, Evan Delay and Tamar Granor, but also because this book represents a great opportunity to provide you with a proven path to improve your experience in going through the certification cycle. A book totally focused on how to prepare for taking the Microsoft Visual FoxPro Certification exam was a key element needed to increase the excitement about the program, and something that we at Microsoft were hoping would happen. This is the first effort that encompasses a complete package that tackles the Visual FoxPro 6.0 Certification exam as a whole, so I congratulate Hentzenwerke Publishing for the initiative and Cindy and Evan for being first.

I truly believe in the countless benefits certification brings to the industry and to the developer community. In this day and age, where hiring managers and business people are looking harder than ever at efficiency and are being very selective at the moment of making hiring decisions, certification comes in as a key standard tool that many of them depend on. Many companies today just review the resumes of people who have a Microsoft Certification under their belt. Microsoft, as a company that's interested in providing standards, has understood this very well; therefore, we have dedicated a lot of resources to the creation, promotion and standardization of the certification program.

Another clear benefit of certification is that it provides individuals with a credential that acknowledges a standard of knowledge in Microsoft products. Certified professionals can show such credentials not only in the presentation of proposals to customers, but also in other promotional activities such as advertising.

Another more subtle but no less important benefit of studying for and taking the certification exam is that the exercise provides a great opportunity to become a better developer. The way the test—and therefore this book—is organized represents a great overview of how to program in Visual FoxPro, as well as how to use features of the product to help with your everyday tasks. I have plenty of testimonials from members of the Visual FoxPro community that prove this. David Stevenson, a good friend and respected member of the Visual FoxPro developer community, said, "I had an intimidating fear of how I measured up as a developer. At the end, the bottom line for me is: It was a great investment of time and energy that I'm happy to have spent, and I'm a much better developer as a result."

As a whole, I consider this book a great reference of programming concepts and practical use of features in Visual FoxPro. I really like the completeness, focus and organization of the chapters. Cindy and Evan have put much effort into showing you what the important concepts are and what the detailed and pertinent information is in the context of the exam. Each chapter has sample questions that provide a flavor of what types of questions appear on the live exam. They have also gone out of their way in recommending a bibliography so that you can deepen your knowledge in the concepts and practices that each chapter brings. Cindy and Evan are also so excited about their in experiences going through the certification process that they want to share them with you, so that you can feel very comfortable with what you need to do. There are plenty of tips on the actual process of taking the test: where to go, how to sign up, even how to use the certification process to your advantage.

I want to congratulate you for buying this book. This moves you one step closer to starting the process of certification. If you decide to take the exam, I want to wish you the best and am certain you'll have a much better chance of passing it because of it. If you're interested in learning how to become a better Visual FoxPro developer without taking the exam, this book will also certainly help. I wouldn't want to finish without congratulating Cindy and Evan for writing this book and adding one more voice encouraging you to take the Visual FoxPro Certification exam as soon as you're ready. Good luck.

Ricardo Wenger
Group Manager
Visual FoxPro Team

Acknowledgements

Professional certification is an issue that is dear to the hearts of a few members of the FoxPro community. We both owe a special debt of gratitude to John Koziol, Ed Rauh, and Whil Hentzen for insisting that this book be written. Thumbsup to Nancy Folsom for starting the study group and keeping it on track, and hats off to Michel Fournier and the Universal Thread, and Steven Black and the FoxWiki for providing venues for us all to learn and share our knowledge. We'd also like to thank the participants in the Visual FoxPro Beta exam study group in the fall of 1999 for stepping up to the plate and supporting the certification process by taking the Beta exams.

Without Tamar Granor, who went way beyond her "Technical Editor" job description, these two newbie authors never would have made it through the writing of this book.

I'd especially like to thank Jim Duffy, who gave me an excellent foundation; Jim Booth, who answered my first newsgroup question and in doing so taught me how to find answers to questions for myself; Anders Altberg, who taught me much of what I know about SQL; and my employer for giving me room to grow.

—*Cindy*

Thanks to my co-author Cindy Winegarden for asking me to participate in the writing of this book. Much gratitude to the following people for advice, code snippets, and other technical input: Craig Berntson, Erik Moore, Bob Tracy, Carl Karsten, and Nick Neklioudov.

—*Evan*

About the Authors

Cindy Winegarden

Cindy Winegarden is the Senior Information Officer for Duke Children's Information Systems, Duke University Medical Center, where she develops applications in Visual FoxPro for Pediatrics Business Office budget and financial statements, decision support ad hoc reporting, and for Duke Children's patient-related statistics and reporting. Cindy was one of the major players in the Fall 1999 VFP Beta Exam Online Study Group, and she edited and posted all of the chat summaries for the group. Cindy is a Universal Thread Visual FoxPro Chat OP, a Microsoft Certified Professional, a conference speaker, and a Microsoft Visual FoxPro MVP. This is Cindy's first book.

Cindy was part of Duke University's first Computer Science graduating class and lives with her family in Durham, North Carolina.

You can reach Cindy at cindy.winegarden@mvps.org.

Evan Delay

Evan Delay is a Visual Studio developer from Vancouver, Canada, who specializes in Visual FoxPro. Evan has been active on the Universal Thread since 1997 and was recently hired as one of its consultants. He helped to organize the VFP exam study groups and currently organizes the Wednesday Night Lectures. In 2000, he was one of the first to earn an MCSD on the VFP track and was named a Visual FoxPro MVP.

You can reach Evan at edelay@universalthread.com.

How to Download the Files

There are two sets of files that accompany this book. The first is the source code referenced throughout the text, and the second is the e-book version of this book—the compiled HTML Help (.CHM) file. Here's how to get them.

Both the source code and the CHM file are available for download from the Hentzenwerke Web site. In order to obtain them, follow these instructions:

1. Point your Web browser to **www.hentzenwerke.com**.

2. Look for the link that says "Download Source Code & .CHM Files." (The text for this link may change over time—if it does, look for a link that references Books or Downloads.)

3. A page describing the download process will appear. This page has two sections:

   - **Section 1:** If you were issued a username/password from Hentzenwerke Publishing, you can enter them into this page.

   - **Section 2:** If you did not receive a username/password from Hentzenwerke Publishing, don't worry! Just enter your e-mail alias and look for the question about your book. Note that you'll need your book when you answer the question.

4. A page that lists the hyperlinks for the appropriate downloads will appear.

Note that the .CHM file is covered by the same copyright laws as the printed book. Reproduction and/or distribution of the .CHM file is against the law.

If you have questions or problems, the fastest way to get a response is to e-mail us at **books@hentzenwerke.com**.

Introduction

Congratulations on your decision to pursue Microsoft professional certification, and thanks for inviting us to come along! While the rest of this book is devoted to covering the knowledge you will need to pass the certification exams, we've devoted this introduction to an overview of the exams and the strategies you need to ensure your success.

We've made this book concise and to-the-point so you can complete your study of the exam topics, rather than running out of time while only partway through. We've seen enough book reviews of other certification study materials that said a particular book didn't cover all of the topics adequately, so we've tried hard to cover every topic, and cover it at the level necessary for success with the exams. We also want to provide you with a study guide that is small enough to take everywhere with you and have available when a spare moment arises, rather than a tome that you can barely carry and never have with you when you wished you did.

Throughout the book, we assumed that you, the reader, have the level of experience with Visual FoxPro that we would expect of a candidate for certification, and have not included a lot of foundational material we anticipate you already know. At the same time, we list other materials you can use to round out your knowledge.

Finally, we included some material here in the introduction on the certification process, why it's important for you to be certified, and how to give yourself every advantage to reach your goals.

Who we are

Although we, Evan and Cindy, have moved forward in our careers since passing the Microsoft Visual FoxPro certification exams, at the time we prepared for, and passed the exams we were just like you, beginning-to-intermediate developers with gaps in our knowledge and experience.

We didn't have the advantage of formal training materials such as this book, so we banded together with other Visual FoxPro developers we met online and made our own. You can see our notes and study materials online on the FoxPro Wiki. In fact, we're so sold on online collaboration that we've done this whole book without ever meeting or speaking on the telephone!

How we started

When Microsoft announced that Visual FoxPro Desktop and Distributed exams would begin their Beta period in a few months, several members of the Visual FoxPro community came together to study online in an organized fashion. A series of chats were held in the Universal Thread chat room several times per week for several weeks, covering both the Desktop and Distributed exams. Evan and Cindy decided to join in, and became acquainted with each other through those chats.

When the study group began, Cindy felt that she was pretty much a VFP and OOP newbie. She'd had some excellent fundamental classroom training, but was mostly still supporting FoxPro for Windows applications. She had been doing SQL and reports in Visual FoxPro for about 10 months. Cindy never passes up an opportunity for free education, so she joined the study group to see what she could pick up and took on the job of editing and posting the logs, thinking that the process of editing would be a good way to work through the material a second time. When she joined the study group, Cindy did not expect to be able to pass the exams before she had several more years of experience.

Cindy took the exams during their Beta period to help provide good statistics for the exam committee, and never expected to pass either exam. She was totally surprised to find that she had passed the Desktop exam and had come close enough on the Distributed exam to know she could pass easily with a little more study when the exam went live in February 2000.

Before the Visual FoxPro exams were announced, Evan had been floundering academically. The old Visual FoxPro 3.0 exams had been retired without a replacement before Evan could take them. To compensate, he decided to get the MCSD certification on the Visual Basic 6.0 track, which meant learning and studying VB at the same time. Not a simple task, and terribly dreary to do alone! Thankfully, at the La Quinta DevCon in June 1999, Microsoft announced that it was developing certification exams for Visual FoxPro 6.0. The dark ages for Evan had ended.

Despite having a good foundation, having used Visual FoxPro since its release, Evan decided he needed to study for the VFP exams. He believed it would solidify his foundation in the language and provide for a jump-start into the MCSD he had been dreaming of. Instead, studying became an eye-opening experience. It quickly exposed areas in which he was weak and areas that he "thought he knew" but that needed more attention. He learned more about areas, like the debugger, that he wasn't using to their fullest potential. The Distributed exam also opened Evan's eyes to the power of technologies like XML, Microsoft Transaction Server, and Distributed COM.

As a result, the two-and-a-half-month period that Evan spent studying for the Visual FoxPro certification exams was one of his most productive learning experiences in Visual FoxPro. Evan's efforts paid off when he passed both Visual FoxPro exams in their Beta period and later achieved his Microsoft Certified Solution Developer status in May 2000.

Who you are

You may be an accomplished Visual FoxPro developer, brushing up on some seldom-used knowledge or technique before taking your exams. You'll be reminding yourself of a few details you might not encounter very often. For example, you could be a developer in a large group who doesn't work with disaster recovery planning because a different department in your organization does that.

You may be a mid-level developer with a few years of experience who feels able to pass the exams with some study, and wants a good formal review. There will be a few areas where you have gaps in your experience, and you'll be using the text and the "Further reading" sections to help identify these areas and fill them in. Perhaps you've never had reason or opportunity to use a COM object. You'll want to make one and see how it behaves when used from inside and outside Visual FoxPro.

You may feel that you're a relative beginner. We encourage you by reminding you that focused effort brings results, and that this book will help you focus your efforts in the right places. You will need to spend a lot of time reading additional materials, experimenting, and augmenting whatever on-the-job experience you already have by working through some examples. In addition to the samples that come with Visual FoxPro on the MSDN

CD, you'll want to check out the links listed on the FoxPro Wiki page (**http://fox.wikis.com/ wc.dll?Wiki~WhereToFindDownloadableVFPSamples**) for pointers to more sample code.

Finally, you may still be sitting on the fence of decision with regard to becoming certified or how many exams to take. Go for it! You'll be glad you did.

You *can* do this!

We encourage you to pursue Microsoft certification. We feel that most developers who pass the Desktop exam should be able to pass the Distributed exam also. Many developers will also be able to pass the Solution Architectures exam (70-100), especially with some preparation. There are study notes for the 70-100 exam on the Wiki that will help with your preparation, and from the book reviews we've read, we feel that the online notes are better than any of the preparation books that are available for that exam!

If you know another language such as Microsoft Visual Basic, have experience with Microsoft SQL Server, or are good with Microsoft Office, it's a short step to Microsoft Certified Solution Developer certification, and we encourage you to polish up your skills and take the fourth exam necessary for this certification.

Microsoft certification brings one more benefit. If you work with at least one other Microsoft Certified Professional, your organization may qualify to be a Microsoft Certified Partner. This program offers several benefits, including the opportunity to register your business with Microsoft, which will make your name available to customers who need services you may offer.

Why get certified?

What motivates you? Each of us has our own "hot buttons" that light the motivational fire under us and push us forward to our goals. Certification is not an easy process. Many of us are already overloaded with a "day job," moonlighting, and "having a life." Making certification a priority will depend on which of several factors motivate you personally, and how much. Try these on for size:

- Knowledge gained from the preparation process

- Self respect from meeting the challenge

- Demonstrated skill

- Demonstrated commitment to your craft

- Inside track to knowledge or services

- Salary increase, promotion

- Edge over uncertified applicants

Ultimately, the exams test the ability to apply skills and knowledge, not personal qualities like creativity, insight, integrity, dependability, or attention to detail. If any of these qualities are severely lacking, the "less qualified" person may actually do the job better than the certified candidate. However, these qualities are difficult to quantify in a resume or personnel folder, while a certification attained against known standards, or the lack of a certification, is easily noted. All other factors being equal, we can't imagine anyone preferring an uncertified candidate!

Certification benefits

Microsoft wants you to be certified, and wants you to continue to be certified. Toward this goal they offer tangible benefits that may motivate you to become certified, and access to materials to help you in your business and business education. Microsoft recognizes and promotes certified individuals as experts with the technical skills and knowledge needed to design, implement, and support solutions with Microsoft products. We'll mention several of these benefits in the sections that follow.

Transcript

A transcript of your certification status and the exams you passed to attain it is available online at the Microsoft Certified Professional (MCP) Web site and is updated shortly after each milestone you attain. The secured area of the MCP Web site includes a "Profile Editor," which you can use to keep your contact information up-to-date, and a transcript tool you can use to print a transcript. There is no mention of the number of tries it took you to pass exams or the fact that you have taken exams that you have not passed. Accessing this site and printing a transcript during a job interview is one way to establish the validity of your Microsoft certification if there is any need to do so. You'll want to be sure your employer always has an updated copy of your transcript.

The transcript lists your name and address, your current certification status (MCP, MCSD, and so forth), the date that status was first achieved, the exams you have passed, and the dates they were passed.

Wallet card, lapel pin

The Microsoft Certified Professional Welcome Kit, which arrives with the first certification, includes a lapel pin and wallet card. These are useful to confirm your certification to clients and employers. Cindy put her pin in the space allotted for such awards on her work ID badge.

Logo

You may use the light blue and white Microsoft Certified Professional or Microsoft Certified Solution Developer logos on your business cards, stationery, and Web pages. Several electronic versions of the artwork are provided, and the program agreement includes guidelines you must adhere to for their use.

Other goodies

The other goodies may change, so we'll just discuss the types of goodies available at the time of this writing. The perks vary by certification level and include things like rebates or discounts on MSDN or MSDN Library subscriptions, access to exclusive benefits on the MCP secured site, access to *MCP Magazine Online's* Premier Area, and discounts from Microsoft partners. You may receive discounts on books and other learning materials, and special invitations to Microsoft conferences, technical training sessions, and special events. You may also purchase clothing, mugs, pens, and other logo items through the MVP Store online.

Leveraging your preparation time

One way to ensure success is to focus your time where it is best spent. You may find that studying is best done as part of a group. It will pay off if you know what Microsoft's point of view is when answering exam questions. Finally, you'll want to know where your strengths and weaknesses are.

Study in groups

We all attended school with other people. Having others along on our educational journey kept us motivated, supplied us with new ideas, and offered a format for discussions. Evan and Cindy found that studying with a group, or even one other person, helped immensely.

Groups offer the opportunity to make yourself accountable to other people for your study. It's not easy to skip studying when another person is waiting for you to check in and report on your assignment. You'll also find that your study partners' motivation level may be high when yours lags behind. Finally, study partners can share complementary knowledge where yours may be lacking.

You may be able to find study partners in your workplace, your local user group, or even online. Cindy prepared for the Solution Architectures exam with someone who was half a world away. Her Sunday evening was his Monday morning! Both Cindy and her study partner passed the Solution Architectures exam.

Know what Microsoft wants

Microsoft begins the process of compiling certification exams by identifying and quantifying which appropriate real-world skills are necessary for developers who provide software solutions, and then translating those skills into a series of exam objectives. Then questions are designed that measure those skills.

The Minimally Qualified Candidate

The Minimally Qualified Candidate is a hypothetical individual whom an employer or customer might consider hiring because of a broad background in a particular technology. Each exam question is evaluated against what experience or knowledge the Minimally Qualified Candidate might be expected to demonstrate related to the skill being measured. The resulting exam is one that the Minimally Qualified Candidate should be expected to pass.

Skills being measured

We'll be discussing the actual skills being measured further on in the "Certification Requirements" section, but let's take a few moments to discuss the focus of the exams. In the past, Microsoft certification exams were full of esoteric knowledge and trick questions. This is no longer the case. You are being certified to do a job, not use a tool, so you won't find questions on where or how to set FWEEK, what the syntax of various commands is, or how to use the wizards. You'll find exam questions that require you to apply skills and knowledge, not merely supply a fact.

Think like Bill
When preparing for and answering exam questions, one should always remember to keep the context of the exam in perspective. Don't expect a BROWSE window to be part of a solution when the Grid control has superseded it. Likewise, expect ADO technology to be a correct answer more often than RDO. In general, know as much as you can about what's "hot" at Microsoft and what techniques are considered "best practice." If you are an isolated developer, take special care to expose yourself to good design and good code online or in magazines.

Know what you do best
We think these exams require a combination of real-world experience, knowledge, and exam skills. Not everyone will have experience with every facet of Visual FoxPro represented in the skills being measured. Besides learning the subjects you aren't familiar with, make sure you know the subjects you have experience with as thoroughly as possible. As with any exam, you can either pass the exam by knowing all the answers for a portion of the topics, or a portion of the answers for all of the topics.

We think it's highly unlikely though that anyone would pass these exams without any real-world experience at all. The exam questions are oriented toward using skills to apply knowledge to a situation that might be encountered in the course of a Visual FoxPro developer's job. Experience gives you practice applying skills in real-world situations, and the exams ask you to apply the same skills to similar situations.

Practice
Be sure to download and practice with the Microsoft demo exams. They will take you through the types of questions and allow you to practice with the exam software. It took Cindy a few tries to get the hang of the drop-and-connect type questions, and she was glad she spent all of those tries at home with a demo exam and not at the exam center with the clock ticking!

The scoring procedures are explained in the demo exams, you'll also see how the timer works, and you'll be able to try out the included calculator. You may even discover some undocumented features like the fact that the items in a tree-type question can be dragged and dropped as well as moved using the mover buttons in the middle.

We can't stress enough how understanding the "mechanics" of these exams and practice with the demos is to your advantage.

Overcoming obstacles
We've already covered the reasons to become certified, in the "Why get certified?" section. Some of you may find that although you want to be certified, there are obstacles to overcome, including finding the time and money it takes to complete the certification process.

Some of you may be long-time, experienced developers who are already well-prepared. You may have an exam voucher, or don't find the exam fee hard to come by. The testing center is nearby. You'll just need to schedule the exam, do a quick review, and get yourself to the testing center.

Some of you may have to travel long distances to take an exam, and use vacation time or lose a day's billable hours to do so. We hope you get there and back safely, and find that the lost hours or lost income was worth it in the long run.

Some of you may find that the exam fee is a lot of money out of a tight budget. Your employer may not be willing to subsidize your certification efforts or may not want to pay for failed exams. You may need your business profits to live on, rather than reinvesting in something like certification. This will be difficult to overcome, but over time, most people can find ways to accumulate extra funds.

Finally, many of you will think that you just don't have time. The real obstacle here is not the time you don't have, but the perception that you don't have it. We challenge you to look for ways you waste time. Dealing with wasted time to recover time for exam preparation will give you new habits that you will find useful after your exams are finished. We also challenge you to examine your priorities. While we don't recommend giving up certain types of things like recreation long-term, attaining a career goal is probably worth giving up television or time at the pub for a few weeks or months.

Scheduling and taking the exams

Exams are given worldwide at Prometric and Virtual University Enterprises testing centers. You can find testing centers and register online, or by telephone. We have heard of problems with the online registration, so you may want to use the Web pages to locate centers in your area, and then register by telephone. Cindy found it easiest to have a list of testing centers in her area, prioritized by location, when registering by phone. That way, when offered a choice between taking the exam Thursday afternoon at test center NC21 or the following Monday morning at center NC36, she could easily visualize the exact locations and make her choice. We recommend confirming the registration with the testing center several days before the exam.

Plan to arrive a little early at the testing center. There may be exams scheduled before or after yours, using the same computer, so you will want to be on time to have all of the allotted time available. The testing center will require you show a photo ID and to leave all your belongings in a secure area before entering the exam room. Restroom breaks while taking exams are usually allowed.

The exam room itself usually has several computers, separated by partitions, and will have pencils and plain paper available for your use during the exam. You will be allowed to take a practice exam to familiarize yourself with the testing software and the types of questions you will encounter. We suggest that you download the Microsoft case study-based demo and one of the free Transcender demos to familiarize yourself with the exam software before you get to the test center. (We feel this is crucial to your success with the 70-100 exam if you are taking that one toward your MCSD certification!)

There is partial credit for "check all that apply" questions, and there are penalties for incorrect answers. If you have no idea of an answer, it's best to skip the question entirely, but if you can narrow down the choices, by all means make an "educated guess."

Your exam will be scored immediately after you finish, and you will see your score on the screen before you leave the exam room. You will also be given a paper score report, which will be your only proof of your score until your Microsoft transcript is updated, usually within a few days after completing the exam.

Use the pencil!

The pencil and paper provided for your use in the exam room are important to your success. Write yourself notes about the questions you want to come back to later. You may not have time to go back to all of the questions, but you can prioritize them and return to those you are most likely to be able to answer.

Be sure to write yourself notes about questions you may have answered incorrectly. Though you are not allowed to take any of these notes out of the exam room, you can read them over carefully before leaving, and write down some notes as soon as you are outside the test center. This is an important tactic for those who may need to take an exam more than once before passing.

Certification requirements

The requirements for each certification level are spelled out on the Microsoft Web site, in addition to other details about the program. There are certification programs for application developers, systems engineers, database analysts, and trainers. Each program is made up of individual exams, any one of which, when passed, confers Microsoft Certified Professional status. The premium certifications—MCSD, MCSE, MCDBA, and MCT—require passing a series of required exams and some electives.

MCSD requirements

The Microsoft Certified Solution Developer certification requires passing one Desktop and one Distributed exam, the Solution Architectures exam, and one of a choice of electives. The Desktop and Distributed exams are offered for each of the core Visual Studio languages, Visual C++, Visual Basic, and Visual FoxPro, and it is not necessary that the Desktop and Distributed exams used to attain MCSD certification be in the same language. Finally, any one of the Desktop or Distributed exams that has not been used as a "core" exam can be used to satisfy the elective requirement.

Exams 70-155 and 70-156

There is a lot of overlap in the Skills Being Measured for the Visual FoxPro Desktop (70-156) and Distributed (70-155) exams, which is why we've covered them together in this book. The real difference between the exams is one of emphasis.

Expect to see more focus on issues related to a small group of users on a LAN, or topics like user services, or visual components on the Desktop exam, and more focus on COM, MTS, and other things you would need for a large number of users on a WAN in the Distributed exam.

Exam 70-100

We should mention the Solution Architectures exam along with our discussion of Visual FoxPro certification. Many Visual FoxPro developers have considerable experience in database design, a large component of the skills being measured by this exam. We encourage all of you to take this exam also, and work toward the premium certification, Microsoft Certified Solution Developer.

We've heard variable reports about how well the commercially available study materials for this exam cover the topic. We think you may be just as well off by working through the discussion on the Wiki and the demo exam, and spend your allotted dollars on taking the exam a second time, if necessary.

Exam retirement

Microsoft retires exams as the technology is outdated or as new technology replaces it. Exam retirement notices are posted well in advance, and certifications are maintained for one full year after an exam is retired. If you have not passed a different exam by that time, your certification will end.

Some developers may be wondering whether they should bypass Visual FoxPro 6.0 certification and be certified under Visual FoxPro 7.0. In our opinion, you shouldn't wait. Exams have not historically been available for every version of FoxPro since the Microsoft certification program began in 1992. Visual FoxPro 6.0 was released with Visual Studio 6.0 in 1998, yet the VFP6 exams did not go live until February 2000. If that pattern continues, exams for VFP7 might not be ready for quite a while.

Finally, there are not huge sweeping changes between Visual FoxPro 6.0 and 7.0. Any time spent preparing yourself for the Visual FoxPro 6.0 exams will make you that much further ahead toward certification in future versions.

Further reading

- Microsoft certification:
  www.microsoft.com/trainingandservices/default.asp?PageID=mcp

- Microsoft Certified Solution Developer program:
  www.microsoft.com/trainingandservices/default.asp?PageID=mcp&PageCall= mcsd&SubSite=cert/mcsd&AnnMenu=mcsd

- Microsoft Certified Solution Developer requirements:
  www.microsoft.com/trainingandservices/default.asp?PageID=mcp&PageCall= requirements&SubSite=cert/mcsd&AnnMenu=mcsd

- Microsoft Certified Partner program: **www.microsoft.com/certpartner/**

- Exam 70-100: "Analyzing Requirements and Defining Solution Architectures for Visual Studio,"
  www.microsoft.com/trainingandservices/exams/examasearch.asp?PageID=70-100

- Exam 70-100 Wiki pages,
  http://fox.wikis.com/wc.dll?Wiki~Exam70-100StudyGuide

- Exam 70-156: "Designing and Implementing Desktop Applications with Microsoft Visual FoxPro® 6.0,"
  www.microsoft.com/trainingandservices/exams/examasearch.asp?PageID=70-156

- Exam 70-156 Wiki pages,
  http://fox.wikis.com/wc.dll?Wiki~Exam70-156StudyGuide

- Exam 70-155: "Designing and Implementing Distributed Applications with Microsoft Visual FoxPro® 6.0," **www.microsoft.com/trainingandservices/exams/examasearch.asp?PageID=70-155**

- Exam 70-155 Wiki pages, **http://fox.wikis.com/wc.dll?Wiki~Exam70-155StudyGuide**

- Exam retirement: **www.microsoft.com/trainingandservices/default.asp?PageID=mcp&PageCall= retired&SubSite=examinfo&AnnMenu=mcdba&AnnLoc=cert/mcdba**

- MCP and MCSD logo merchandise: **www.mvpstore.com/default.asp**

Testing centers

- Prometric Online Registration: **www.2test.com/index.jsp**

- Virtual University Enterprises: **www.vue.com/ms/**

Exam demos

- Microsoft demos, especially the case study-based test demo: **www.microsoft.com/trainingandservices/default.asp?PageID=mcp&PageCall= tesinn&SubSite=examinfo**

- Transcender demos: **www.transcender.com/products/demos.asp**

Chapter 1
Developing the Conceptual and Logical Design

You can't reach a destination without knowing what it is. Furthermore, without a roadmap, your route may be inefficient or you may never reach your goal. Even if you know both of these, without good communication during the journey, misunderstandings can arise among the participants. Can this be said more succinctly? Know where you want to go, how to get there and that everyone understands these two items. Conceptual and logical designs are tools to take a project from an idea and turn it into a plan of action.

Before delving into the specifics of conceptual and logical designs, let's look at the larger picture of software design. Most fundamentally, why are we even doing this project? Four words: to solve a problem. As Booth and Sawyer say in *Effective Techniques for Application Development with Visual FoxPro 6.0*, "The client has a problem that is causing them pain… they are hiring us to relieve their pain." Sometimes the client isn't clear as to whatthe problem is, and we must help them to define it. Once this is done, we begin to formulate a plan (or design) to solve the problem.

Here is an example of an ill-defined problem that then leads to a poor solution. Suppose your two children are given a school assignment of bringing a dessert they have made to class. You show them where all of the ingredients are and then retire to your home office to finish writing a chapter of your latest book. Within a few minutes, you hear the sounds of arguing and a loud crash. You dash into the kitchen only to find both kids rolling around on the floor in a pitched battle for a lemon. You grab the lemon and demand an explanation from each. Both plead that they need the lemon for their recipe. Frustrated (and behind on adeadline), you grab a knife, cut the coveted fruit in half, and hand a portion to each child. The next day, each child returns with a failing grade on their assignment because their desserts tasted funny.

On further investigation, you find that one childneeded only the peel of a lemon to make some zest, while the other needed the juice. You failed to help the clients (the children) realize what they really needed. They thought lemon, but they really needed apart of the lemon. Accepting an incorrect statement of the problem caused you to reach a solution that did not solve the problem. In addition, you failed to determine that using half a lemon ruined both recipes because they tasted bland.

Why create a design for a project?

- To clearly define the problem.

- To clearly define the solution to the problem. Without a clear goal, a project can flounder because it will be hard to determine whether a project has succeeded or not.

- To help estimate the resources needed to accomplish the goal.

- To assist in discovering the best way of achieving the goal of the project.

- To discover flaws with the original idea. Discovering problems early helps to solve them or minimize their impact.

- To facilitate communication between the developer and client, as well as among members of the development team.

The three phases of design are the conceptual, logical, and physical designs. Conceptual design is a high-level overview of the project that, in general, is in plain English, perhaps with a few diagrams. The logical design goes into more detail by breaking the conceptual design into services or components. The physical design then maps the architecture of the logical design into actual hardware and software.

Conceptual design

The conceptual design is a high-level overview of the problem and how to solve it. This can be as simple as a paragraph or a page of text. Then list the high-level requirements specified by the user. This can be as simple as a table in Microsoft Word. It may also include diagrams or tables that show usage scenarios. (Formalized usage scenarios are called "use cases.") Once again, these are meant to be simple and only give the overview.

The document should be understandable by non-technical people. You don't want to confuse your client with technical jargon because this could lead to misunderstandings, and a misunderstanding during this early stage could lead to disastrous results, as we saw with the lemon incident. In addition, no particular hardware or software should be mentioned—this will be decided during the physical design phase.

How do you create a conceptual design? Meet with the users of the system. Ask them questions about their business and how they do their current tasks, summarize the results, and have them review it. Repeat this process until each of you feels comfortable that the problem has been described. In addition, you may also want to follow users around to observe how they get information and accomplish tasks. Sometimes details might be so obvious to them that they forget to mention them in an interview.

Here's an overview description of a project that is included in the conceptual design:

The owner of an insurance business wants to automate her business. The main reason is that claims adjusters aren't being notified of claims promptly. This is because the insurance agents are very busy and only have time to look up the claims adjuster for a territory (in a thick manual) at the end of the day. Notifying claims adjusters via e-mail will allow customers' claims to be paid more quickly.

- *Agents will start policies for new customers.*

- *Agents will modify existing policies by adding or removing vehicles from the policy.*

- *Agents will look up policies by policy number or customer's last name.*

- *The agent can then print a bill for the customer.*

- *The agent will also input insurance claims when an automobile is damaged. By law, a claim must include the date of the incident, the part that was damaged, and the type of the event (crash, break-in or other).*

- *When the claim is filed, the application sends e-mail to the claims adjuster that covers the territory where the customer lives.*

The next part of the conceptual design is the list of requirements. These are extracted from the overview paragraph and from the interviews with the client. More details will be added in the logical design. **Table 1** shows the requirements for our insurance example.

Table 1. *List of requirements gathered during the conceptual design phase.*

1	New policies shall be entered into the system.
2	Vehicles shall be added to and deleted from the policy.
3	A statement shall be printed when a new policy is completed or a policy has been modified.
4	A policy shall be retrieved by policy number or customer's last name.
5	An adjuster can only work on claims where the customer lives in his or her territory.
6	Claims shall be entered into the system.
7	When a claim has been entered, the system will e-mail the adjuster who covers the territory in which the customer lives. The e-mail will contain the details of the claim.
8	Agents are paid on commission; an agent's name must be associated with the policy when it is created.

Next, the scenarios are listed. Each scenario documents how a user interacts with the system and shows the system's responses. These scenarios are derived from the requirements list. For brevity, **Table 2** shows only the case when a new policy is entered.

Table 2. *Scenario for the creation of a new policy.*

Action	Software reaction
The customer phones or walks into insurance office to start a new policy. The agent starts a new policy.	An entry form is displayed for the customer and vehicle information.
The customer verbally gives personal and vehicle information. The agent puts this information into the form.	The system determines the rate based on the model year and prints a bill.

This completes the conceptual design. Notice that non-technical people can understand the resulting document. As we expand upon this design in the logical design, the user may need some assistance in learning how to decipher the information.

Logical design

The logical design breaks down the conceptual design into components and services. Once again, it is important to stress that the logical design does not specify particular hardware or software that will be used in the final solution. For example, the same logical design could be used to create a physical design for an Oracle database, a VFP database or a non-relational data store. Leave technology decisions for the physical design stage. The logical design can be communicated via use case diagrams, data flow diagrams, and object diagrams.

N-tier design is a useful model for an application design. It breaks the components into at least three layers, which are typically called the interface, business logic tier, and data tier. You may see these called by slightly different names in other texts, but the idea is the same. N-tier design is in contrast to single-tier design, where all services are mixed together, and two-tier (also known as client/server) design, where the user interface is separated from data, but the business rules are spread over both tiers. N-tier design does not mean that our solution will use COM components or have separate .EXE or .DLL files. N-tier design is simply a logical separation of the components or services that may or may notend up being separate physical components.

A very common design for n-tier applications divides the responsibilities into the following layers:

- The interface layer, which contains components that the user or another system will interact with. Examples include an invoice data entry form and a password dialog.

- The business layer, which contains services that are not directly accessed by the user, but that the system carries out based on user interaction with the interface layer. This is where the business logic or business rules are found. In *Advanced Object Oriented Programming with Visual FoxPro 6.0*, Markus Egger indicates that the right side of the use case table contains hints as to the business objects. A credit card validation module is an example.

- The data layer, which contains entities (nouns) that are found through the conceptual design. These will be things such as invoices, customers, and credit cards. The data layer interacts only with the business layer, never with the interface layer.

Object modeling is one form of modular design that fits well with n-tier design. As each object is defined, it is put into one of the three tiers. Nouns tend to be objects, while verbs are usually methods of the objects. For instance, from our insurance use cases wecan derive the objects shown in **Figure 1**.

Interface objects
Policy entry form
Claim entry form
Policy lookup form

Business objects
Bill printer
Policy rate calculator
Claim mailer

Data objects
Customer
Policy
Vehicle
Agent
Claims adjuster
Claim

Figure 1. Objects grouped into three tiers.

The next step is to determine the properties of the objects. Properties are descriptive data about an object. For example, the Claim object would have the following properties: DateOfIncident, PartDamaged, ClaimType and PolicyId.

At this point, you also determine the methods of objects. Methods are the verbs that are found in the use cases. For instance, the Bill Printer object would have a PrintBill() method.

We have kept this section on logical design simple and avoided a discussion of modeling notation that is a book in itself. The reader is urged to read more about use cases and the Unified Modeling Language (UML). Markus Egger's *Advanced Object Oriented Programming with Visual FoxPro 6.0* and Steven Black's **http://fox.wikis.com** are great resources for more information.

In the next chapter, we will discuss the logical data model, which focuses on relational design rather than object design.

Sample Question

Which of the following should be included in a conceptual design?

A. Database diagrams
B. Listing of the stored procedures to be used in SQL Server
C. The version of browser to be supported
D. An overview of how an order is filled

Answer: D

Further reading

Design

- *Advanced Object Oriented Programming with Visual FoxPro 6.0*, Markus Egger, Chapter 12, "The Unified Modeling Language"

- *Advanced Object Oriented Programming with Visual FoxPro 6.0*, Markus Egger, Chapter 13, "Collecting Requirements"

- *Advanced Object Oriented Programming with Visual FoxPro 6.0*, Markus Egger, Chapter 14, "Analyzing the Problem"

- *Effective Techniques for Application Development with Visual FoxPro 6.0*, Jim Booth and Steve Sawyer, Chapter 1, "In the Beginning"

- *Effective Techniques for Application Development with Visual FoxPro 6.0*, Jim Booth and Steve Sawyer, Chapter 8, "Managing Business Logic—N-Tier System Design"

- *Internet Applications with Visual FoxPro 6*, Rick Strahl, Chapter 11, "The Development Process"

- "Using a Three-Tier Architecture Model," **http://msdn.microsoft.com/library/default.asp?URL=/library/psdk/cossdk/ pgdistributed_design_9lik.htm**

- *Visual Basic 6 Distributed Exam Cram*, Michael Lane Thomas and Dan Fox, Chapter 2, "Distributed Application Design"

- **http://fox.wikis.com/wc.dll?Wiki~LogicalModel**

Object-oriented design

- *Advanced Object Oriented Programming with Visual FoxPro 6.0,* Markus Egger, Chapter 1, "Basic Concepts"

- *Advanced Object Oriented Programming with Visual FoxPro 6.0*, Markus Egger, Chapter 8, "The Bigger Picture"

- *Advanced Object Oriented Programming with Visual FoxPro 6.0*, Markus Egger, Chapter 9, "Three-Tiered Development"

- *Advanced Object Oriented Programming with Visual FoxPro 6.0*, Markus Egger, Chapter 15, "Object Modeling"

Chapter 2
Developing a Logical
Data Model

Data is the heart of our Visual FoxPro applications. Getting data safely stored and updated in our databases is our "bread and butter." Crucial to doing this is good design for our data model. We need to understand the difference between the logical data model, discussed here, and the physical data model, discussed in Chapter 8, "Creating a Physical Database," as we move through this design process. Without good design, we'll always be fighting the awkwardness and integrity problems to which poor design gives rise.

Dr. Edgar F. Codd's landmark paper, "A Relational Model of Data for Large Shared Data Banks," was published in *Communications of the Association for Computing Machinery* in June 1970. In it he gave us a definition of a good database structure and a process for "normalizing" our data by sequentially applying rules to the tables or "entities." Others, including Raymond F. Boyce, joined Codd in refining the definition and the process of normalizing the data.

The goal of data normalization is to avoid problems caused by poor design of the database. Every type of duplicate data and every type of dependency adds complexity to our database that could easily be avoided by better design. Let's avoid patched, duct-taped spaghetti code from the beginning by understanding the rules of normalization and applying them. In addition to the normalization process, we should also understand the circumstances where it makes sense to denormalize our data.

Part of the difference between the "logical" data model, which we are discussing here, and the "physical" data model, discussed in Chapter 8, "Creating a Physical Database," is the way we think of key fields. In the logical model, we think of key fields as a way to logically join tables. In the physical database, we use these logical keys as the basis for our index expressions.

Normalization rules

Applying "rules" to the data in a sequential fashion carries out the process of table normalization. Then, if there are specific reasons, the data may be denormalized. Here's a statement of the rules, with more detailed explanations following:

- First Normal Form: There should be no repeating fields in the table.

- Second Normal Form: The table is in 1NF, and all non-key fields depend on the whole primary key for their value.

- Third Normal Form: The table is in 2NF, and there is no co-dependence between non-key fields.

- Boyce-Codd Normal Form: The table is in Boyce-Codd Normal Form if it is in 3NF for any fields that are alternate candidate keys.

- Fourth Normal Form: The table is in 3NF, and it has no independently multi-valued primary keys.

- Fifth Normal Form: The table is in 5NF if it is in 4NF and there are no pairwise cyclical relationships in primary keys that have three or more components.

What's really important here is not some academic definition of normalization rules, but how we should design our databases under these rules.

First Normal Form (1NF)

Normalizing a table to 1NF means that fields with repeating values should not be allowed, but should be moved to a different table. Cindy's automobile insurance company's database is an example of data that is not in 1NF. When her third teenager's car was added to the insurance policy, Cindy wondered why she started getting two insurance bills to pay. The insurance company only had room for four automobiles on one policy. Guess why! **Figure 1** shows what Cindy imagines their table design looked like.

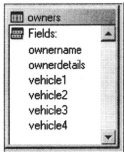

Figure 1. Non-normalized table limiting a policy to four vehicles.

The solution to this problem is to leave the policy owner's demographic information in the Owners table and move the automobiles on the policy to a Vehicles table. The automobiles would then be associated with the policy owner in the Owners table through an OwnerID primary key, as shown in **Figure 2**.

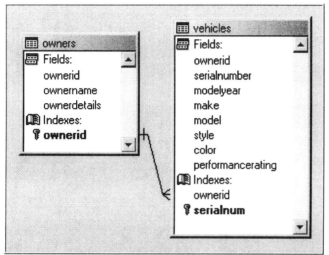

Figure 2*. Owner and vehicle data in first normal form. Policy owners may have as many vehicles as necessary on one policy. It is difficult, however, to change the performance rating of all vehicles of this ModelYear/Make/Model when the tables are not normalized.*

Second Normal Form (2NF)

A table in 2NF must not have fields that do not depend on the whole primary key for their value. Suppose the insurance company kept track of "high-performance" cars because their drivers exhibited more "risky" driving behavior and should have a different insurance rate. Their Vehicles table currently stores OwnerID, SerialNumber, ModelYear, Make, Model, Style, Color and PerformanceRating. The primary key in this table is SerialNumber. While ModelYear and Color are both dependent on SerialNumber, PerformanceRating depends only on ModelYear, Make and Model.

The insurance company might decide that Cindy's 1996 magenta Neon Sport's PerformanceRating is really more like that of the Neon ACR than the basic Neon model and wish to change the insurance rate on all Neon Sport vehicles. In the current schema (see Figure 2), they would need to change all records with ModelYear/Make/Model = "1996/Plymouth/Neon Sport" to PerformanceRating = "High."

A properly normalized database (see **Figure 3**) would have a Model table where the PerformanceRating was stored. The insurance company would only need to change the value of PerformanceRating once in the Model table to adjust every policy owner's rate for owners of that type of vehicle.

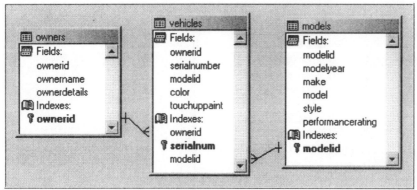

Figure 3. *Owner and vehicle data in second normal form—it's easy to change the performance rating of a particular vehicle type when the tables are normalized.*

Third Normal Form (3NF)

Tables in 3NF do not have dependencies between non-key fields. Suppose the insurance company stored the touch-up paint color number for Cindy's Neon in the Vehicles table (see Figure 3) in case the vehicle was damaged. The data is not normalized because TouchUpPaint is not dependent on either key field. In **Figure 4**, the touch-up paint color number is only dependent upon the ColorID field and has been moved to a table other than the Vehicles table, normalizing the schema again.

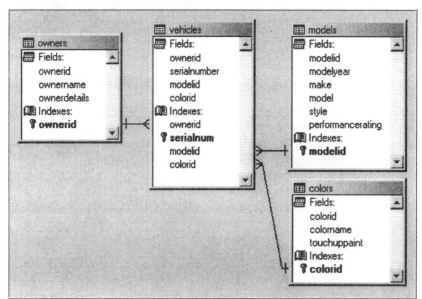

Figure 4. *Owner and vehicle data in 3NF—the logical data model is normalized when TouchUpPaint color number depends only upon a key field in the table where the value is kept.*

Many people stop at 3NF in designing their databases, and in fact only more complex databases need to deal with forms beyond 3NF.

Boyce-Codd Normal Form (BCNF)

Boyce-Codd Normal Form deals with the existence of candidate keys. Suppose automobile manufacturers imprinted a unique number on the engine block as it came off the line and the insurance company added this field to their Vehicles table. Because each vehicle already has a unique SerialNumber and can have only one EngineBlockID, either could be removed and the table would still be in 3NF. Specifying that EngineBlockID must be unique and that the table must be in 3NF when EngineBlockID is the primary key puts this table in Boyce-Codd Normal Form.

Fourth Normal Form (4NF)

Fourth Normal Form requires that the table have no independently multi-valued primary keys. Suppose the insurance company is planning their BookValue table. Shown in **Figure 5**, it contains the ModelYear, Make, Model, Transmission, Style, OptionPackage and BookValue. The first six fields together (ModelYear + Make + Model + Transmission + Style + OptionPackage) comprise the primary key—you need all six to access the BookValue. Transmission, Style and OptionPackage are each independent multi-valued attributes of ModelYear + Make + Model.

ModelYear	Make	Model	Transmission	Style	Optionpackage	Bookvalue
1996	Plymouth	Neon Sport	Manual	Sedan	Regular	7090.0000
1996	Plymouth	Neon Sport	Manual	Sedan	Deluxe	8490.0000
1996	Plymouth	Neon Sport	Manual	Coupe	Regular	7040.0000
1996	Plymouth	Neon Sport	Manual	Coupe	Deluxe	8440.0000

Figure 5. Transmission, Style and OptionPackage are independently multi-valued attributes of ModelYear + Make + Model. What happens when we want to add BookValue data for Automatic transmissions?

If the insurance company needed to add the "Automatic" transmission to the table, they would need to add one record for each combination of Style + OptionPackage as shown in **Figure 6**.

You can put a table like this into 4NF by creating multiple tables to handle the different multi-valued components. That means creating separate tables (see **Figure 7**) for the value added to the BookValue by each of the Transmissions, Styles, and OptionPackages choices. Those who have ever read *Kelly's Blue Book* are familiar with value being added to a base price for each of these.

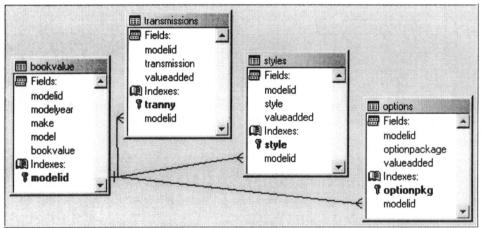

Modelyear	Make	Model	Transmission	Style	Optionpackage	Bookvalue
1996	Plymouth	Neon Sport	Manual	Sedan	Regular	7090.0000
1996	Plymouth	Neon Sport	Manual	Sedan	Deluxe	8490.0000
1996	Plymouth	Neon Sport	Manual	Coupe	Regular	7040.0000
1996	Plymouth	Neon Sport	Manual	Coupe	Deluxe	8440.0000
1996	Plymouth	Neon Sport	Automatic	Sedan	Regular	7625.0000
1996	Plymouth	Neon Sport	Automatic	Sedan	Deluxe	9025.0000
1996	Plymouth	Neon Sport	Automatic	Coupe	Regular	7575.0000
1996	Plymouth	Neon Sport	Automatic	Coupe	Deluxe	8975.0000

Figure 6. In order to add BookValue data for vehicles with Automatic transmissions, we need to add a total of four records to this table for each ModelYear + Make + Model combination.

Figure 7. Vehicle options normalized to Fourth Normal Form. Each multi-valued component, and the value it adds to the BookValue of the vehicle, is stored in its own table.

Fifth Normal Form (5NF)

A table in 5NF must not have pairwise cyclical dependencies of the primary key that are composed of three or more component fields. This deals with the situation of a table whose primary key is composed of three or more fields, an easy occurrence in a many-to-many table like what the insurance company might see when processing a claim.

Suppose that the insurance company has a table for processing claims that matches Branch Offices, Claims Adjusters and Outside Agencies. When a new Adjuster is employed, serving all branch offices in the state, a record needs to be added for each combination of outside agencies. For any one value, you always need to know the other two values in order to define a record. The solution to this problem is to separate the Outside Agencies into its own table that has a many-to-many relationship with the OfficesAdjusters table.

An even better plan is to separate all three types of data into BranchOffices, ClaimsAdjusters and OutsideAgencies. Then, when a claim is processed, it can have a foreign key to the BranchOffices to show which office handled it, a foreign key to the ClaimsAdjusters to show which adjuster was assigned, and the ClaimID can be a foreign key in the ClaimsAgencies table, which serves as a junction between the claim and the OutsideAgencies involved.

Most of us never see these 4NF and 5NF problems occurring, because our design was done properly from the beginning! In general, we should not be "penny wise and pound foolish" about adding an additional field to a table to serve as a primary key, eliminating the need to deal with keys made up of several values combined together.

The primary key

The primary key is a value that uniquely defines a record. It can be numeric or character, a single value or a combination of several values. In Visual FoxPro, we can define a Primary index on a field in a table within a .DBC and the FoxPro data engine will automatically prevent us from entering any duplicate values. We can have only one Primary index, but for other fields that could be used as a primary key—for example, the EngineBlockID field mentioned earlier—we could specify that the field have a Candidate index. FoxPro gives us the same benefit for a Candidate index as for the Primary index—it prevents the entry of duplicate values.

In practice, the primary key should never be meaningful, real-world data that the user enters. No Social Security numbers, no traffic ticket numbers and so forth. Cindy's middle child went through half his life with the wrong SSN, and Cindy had quite a time getting things corrected in several systems that disregarded this rule!

We will discuss primary keys further in Chapter 8, "Creating a Physical Database."

Relationships

Entity relationships fall into three categories: one-to-one, one-to-many and many-to-many.

One-to-one relationships

One does not see the one-to-one relationship often in database design. Any tables with a one-to-one relationship between their records could logically be combined into one larger table. Reasons for separating the tables might include the need to make a very large table smaller, to have more than FoxPro's 254 fields, or to avoid keeping seldom-used data open and available while an application is running. As you can see, these constraints come into play when the logical database design is translated into the physical database design.

One-to-many relationships

One-to-many relationships are at the heart of relational database design. They are often called "parent-child" or "master-slave" relationships. We see these relationships in our everyday lives. For example, there are natural one-to-many relationships between customers and orders, orders and line items, installment loans and monthly payments, and the Owners and Vehicles tables in the insurance company examples described earlier.

Many-to-many relationships

We also see many-to-many relationships in our daily lives. Teachers and students, physicians and patients, library materials and patrons, and parts and orders are all examples we are familiar with. Data for instances of a many-to-many relationship is housed in a type of table called a junction, or linking, table. Sometimes all this table contains are the primary keys of each of the tables it is joining, and other times it contains additional data. For example, many library patrons may borrow and return many books. After each return, the condition of the book may be noted. The junction table would contain the book key, the patron key, the borrow and return dates, and the condition of the book when it was returned.

In our insurance company example, the Vehicles table (see Figure 4) is a junction table for the many models and many colors possible in the vehicles covered by the company's policies. It stores additional information, including the policy owner and serial number of the vehicle in question.

A many-to-many relationship can be thought of as a combination of two one-to-many relationships. One merely needs to put blinders on and look only one way out of the junction table to avoid confusion.

Foreign keys

A foreign key is a field in the current table that holds the values of the primary key of another table. In the child table, the foreign key field contains the primary key of the child record's parent record. Foreign keys are used to define relationships among tables and in the JOINs of views. A junction table may contain only two fields, both of which are foreign keys. Because it is a junction table, it essentially has two parent tables. Again, let us mention that primary and foreign keys are used to define logical relationships in the logical data model and to define indexes in the physical data model. Visual FoxPro uses indexes to carry out the business of persistent logical relationships between tables.

Referential integrity

Referential integrity refers to the validity of relationships between entities in a database. A database can be said to have referential integrity when there are no unmatched foreign key values. That means that there will never be a "dead link" between a foreign key in one table and a record in the table where the foreign key is primary. Broken referential integrity—for example, deleting a parent record when there are child records present—leaves what are commonly called "orphan" child records.

FoxPro provides us with database insert, update and delete triggers that allow us to cascade changes made in a parent record to all of the child records. (The same triggers also allow us to prevent those changes in the parent should that be our choice.) These database capabilities make enforcing referential integrity much easier than hand-coding each time and in each part of the application that contains code to insert, update or delete records. These triggers will be discussed more in Chapter 8, "Creating a Physical Database," where we go into detail about physical design issues.

Business rules, data integrity and the data model

The business rules for data integrity are a part of the logical design. When the insurance company transfers a claims adjuster from the Northern territory to the Southern territory, what should happen to the outstanding claims left in the Northern territory? The customer would sensibly tell us that the claims overseen by the adjuster should not be deleted from the database when the adjuster is deleted from the list of adjusters who are active in the Northern territory. This would lead to orphan child records. They might prefer to keep the adjuster active in the Northern territory until all of his claims are resolved, transfer the claims to the Southern territory with the adjuster even though the addresses aren't in the south, or transfer the claims to another adjuster who is active in the Northern territory.

The customer might even dictate that the child records be ignored when the parent record is deleted. It might be acceptable to the public library to have orphan borrowing transactions for a book that can no longer be identified, but we would advise the insurance company that their clients would not be happy should their claim records become orphan children assigned to no claims adjuster!

The types of rules mentioned previously are "row-level" rules because they are applied to a whole record of data at one time. There are also business rules for individual fields. For example, in the physical data model, it makes sense to specify that the insured value of an automobile cannot be blank or a negative number. A business rule for the insured value of an automobile, determined by the insurance company, might specify that the insured value of an automobile can only be equal to Blue Book value if the customer has purchased the "Basic" or "Standard" insurance options, and that no towing claims can be filed by customers who have not purchased towing insurance.

Business rules for data integrity float in a "gray area" between the logical and physical designs, and in a "gray area" between the presentation tier and the data tier of the application. You'll find that many of the topics we mention here will be covered again in Chapter 8, "Creating a Physical Database."

Denormalization

Denormalization is the process of "breaking the rules" for a specific reason. Reasons to denormalize include:

- Reporting
- Data warehousing
- Performance

Denormalization for reporting

The first and most obvious situation we think of when we denormalize data is for purposes of reporting. When we create a view or select data into a cursor for our reports, we fill in all of the parent data, lookup values and so on, so they will be readily available for presentation. This is not "real" denormalization, though, because the data does not persist in this format after we have presented it to the user.

Denormalization for data warehousing

Data in a warehouse is usually static. An example of this is the decision support database Cindy uses to track trends in the hospital where she works. Last month's physician productivity figures are "old news" in the sense that there will be no more activity added after the closing date. Since Cindy and other users access this data often, and usually in the same way, the DBA keeps a denormalized copy of the data available, speeding up queries. Since the data is mostly static, there aren't problems with updating the non-normalized fields when the source data changes.

Denormalization for performance

A fully normalized database might require many JOINs among its tables on the way to constructing views that are commonly used by the application. JOINs can be costly in time and server resources, and selective denormalizing can really be beneficial. Perhaps the insurance company will want to see the performance rating of a vehicle every time the policy information for that vehicle is accessed. They know that performance ratings won't change often, and they want to be able to bring up policy information as quickly as possible when an agent is on the telephone with a customer. Storing the performance rating in the Vehicles table would result in denormalized data, but it would add a significant gain in access time. The downside—having to update the Vehicles table appropriately when the performance rating for a particular vehicle changes—seems a small tradeoff.

Sample Questions

The purpose of a foreign key is to:
  A. Define the relationship of the current table with a table containing foreign-language translations of all the data in the current table.
  B. Define the relationship of records in the current table with their child records in the child table.
  C. Define the relationship of records in the current table with their parent records in the parent table.
  D. Get you into the washroom in the Embassy.

  Answer: C

The insurance company needs to assign claims to categories for the home office, the traffic safety board and the vehicle safety board to track factors involved. Each of the agencies that wants category assignments has its own list of factors to be evaluated for each claim. The insurance company "doesn't want anything complicated" and suggests some logical-value columns added to the Claims table denoting such categories as "weather," "vehicle malfunction" and so on. You tell them that there will always be new categories to add, that each of the outside agencies will have its own definition of "weather" or "vehicle malfunction," and that these may change over time. You also tell them that table structure changes are costly.
  You recommend:
  A. Adding a ClaimType column to the Claims table and adding a Factors table with a one-to-many relationship between the FactorID and the ClaimType in the Claims table.
  B. Adding a Factors table and a junction table with columns FactorID and SerialNumber creating a many-to-many relationship between the Factors table and the Vehicles table.

C. Adding a Factors table and a junction table with FactorID and ClaimID creating a many-to-many relationship between the Factors table and the Claims table.
D. Adding a Factors table and a FactorAgencies table with a many-to-one relationship between the AgencyID foreign key in the Factors table and the AgencyID in the Agencies table.

Answer: C

You see design flaws in the examples at the beginning of this chapter. You are ready to write to the authors, saying that:
A. Using the vehicle SerialNumber as a primary key in the Vehicles table breaks the rule about using a meaningful value as a primary key.
B. Using the vehicle SerialNumber as a primary key in the Vehicles table breaks the rule about using a user-entered value as a primary key.
C. The primary keys of the Transmissions, Styles and Options tables are ModelID + either Transmission, Style or OptionPackage, and multi-part primary keys may cause problems later on. A single numeric or character value would be a better choice.
D. A and B only.
E. A, B, and C.

Answer: E

Further reading

- *Joe Celko's SQL For Smarties: Advanced SQL Programming, Second Edition*, Joe Celko, Chapter 2, "Normalization"

- *Effective Techniques for Application Development with Visual FoxPro 6.0*, Jim Booth and Steve Sawyer, Appendix Two, "Relational Database Design"

Chapter 3
Deriving the Physical Design

The physical design is concerned with taking the entities developed in the logical design and mapping these to a specific technology. The hardware and software that are chosen are influenced by the reality of the environment as we near implementation. This chapter looks at the ways we divide our application into tiers and some of the issues related to class libraries and components.

We saw previously that the logical design did not mention specific hardware and software because this allows the logical design to be more versatile. The same logical design can be used for a pure VFP project or a Web-based SQL Server project. This could save our skins at this stage if the client's business environment changes, the project budget is cut in half (we can no longer use SQL Server) or our Oracle DBA leaves the company. With no hardware and software specifics in the logical model, we're well positioned to embark on a different physical design based on these new circumstances.

As we move from the logical to the physical design, we should think of our project as a series of relatively separate and distinct parts or tiers. While the usual distribution of the application is a user interface tier, a business tier, and a data tier, there can be any number of tiers.

Microsoft's Component Object Model (COM) provides a lot of flexibility and a good match for implementing our object-oriented n-tier logical data model. COM allows a developer to expose objects written in a variety of programming languages to other programming languages and software. COM allows us to deploy an application on a single client computer or across several servers via Distributed COM (DCOM). (For a more complete discussion of COM, see Chapter 6, "Creating and Managing COM Components.") One of our favorite aspects of COM components written in Visual FoxPro is that we create them the same way as non-component classes; to turn a class into a component, we only need to add the OLEPUBLIC keyword!

Design considerations

In mapping our logical design to a physical design, we need to think of four factors: performance, maintainability, extensibility, and availability. Often we are balancing these four criteria against each other, and we will need to apply some general principles to our specific situation. High performance may come at a cost of lower maintainability. Fortunately, Visual FoxPro is a flexible tool. We'll see how these criteria lead us away from using a single monolithic design to dividing our project into a user interface tier, a business tier and a data tier.

Performance

Performance is the responsiveness of the system, and performance is relative. For instance, having a month-end accounting routine that takes several hours to run may not be a problem, but making a customer on the Web wait more than a few seconds may be a critical issue. How does performance affect the physical implementation? If the application is to be used by only one person on a single computer, we may decide to implement it with Visual FoxPro alone, where all of the tiers are compiled into one EXE. Accessing an object within an EXE, hosted on a local hard drive, is much faster than accessing the same object as a DCOM component on an overworked corporate server. Conversely, if an invoice component requires a lot of complex calculations, we might decide to host the component via DCOM on a server so that the user's computer won't be tied up during the long complex calculations.

Maintainability

Maintainability is the ease of making changes to the system. In a large monolithic application with a formal testing process, one change might require retesting, recompiling, and redeploying the whole system. To increase maintainability, we may want to divide our application into a series of smaller pieces, and thus only need to retest and redeploy the one piece that has changed. If we use DCOM and host all of our components centrally on a server, we would only need to change one component and retest that piece and redeploy to one server machine. That sure beats taking the whole system offline or visiting each workstation to update the software!

Extensibility

Extensibility is the ability to enhance a system without having to completely change it. For instance, we might want to design our component so that it can be scaled from 10 users to 1,000 easily. In addition, we may want our tax object to be able to handle any new countries in which we open offices.

Availability

Availability indicates the time a system is up and running. For example, a company may choose to centralize a database for an international company in one city. All branch offices then access the data via the Internet. This increases maintainability because there's only one database application to maintain. However, it may decrease availability due to communication problems using the Internet. This is especially true in developing countries that have a poor telecommunications infrastructure. The outlying office would be cut off from the data.

An example with COM

COM and DCOM architectures give the Visual FoxPro developer flexibility in deploying a solution and in addressing the performance, maintainability, extensibility, and availability of a solution. When used in conjunction with n-tier architecture, they are even more powerful.

For example, say we build a stand-alone application for a sales manager in a small company so she can keep track of her sales. Being smart developers, we design it to be three-tiered using COM components. The VFP front end calls a business-layer middle-tier COM component, which then calls a data services back-end COM component, which interacts with the data itself. All of this is resident on the sales manager's hard drive, but she does daily backups, so all is well.

Then, suppose the company is doing well and hires more sales staff. We make some minor modifications to the system so that we can handle multiple salespeople and host it on an NT server.

Soon the company expands nationally, and we change our middle tier to DCOM so that it can access components over the Internet. As the business grows, we change the front end to use a plain browser to remove the need for local staff to do any workstation installs. We also move the business layer onto one server running COM+ (formerly Microsoft Transaction Server) to help with the traffic, and the data into Microsoft SQL Server on another server to improve performance.

As we can see by the contrived but perhaps not unrealistic example, we made our system extensible by using COM to allow scalability. We have increased performance by allowing components to be run on different servers. We increased maintainability by centralizing the business and data services in the main office (hopefully) near the IS staff.

Availability of this system is double-pronged. On one hand, we have increased system availability by hosting the middle (business) tier and data tiers on reliable servers. On the other hand, the remote offices are vulnerable to potential communication outages by using the public Internet. One way to increase availability is to have an NT or Windows 2000 server at each local office that's synchronized with the main server each night. If the main server is unavailable, the application can switch to this local copy of the data and business can resume. The downside is that the application, data synchronization, and hardware become more complex and could make the system more difficult and more expensive to maintain. These are issues that we need to discuss with our clients to determine which path is most important or appropriate for them.

Class libraries

In Visual FoxPro, the building blocks we need for our application's objects are called classes. Object-oriented classes have the following characteristics:

- Inheritance

- Encapsulation

- Delegation

- Containership

- Polymorphism

Inheritance

Inheritance allows a class to be defined based on another class called its parent class or superclass. The parent class is more general in nature, while the child class is more specific. The child class inherits all of the properties and methods of the parent class. For example, suppose we subclassed a text box class to handle date format and validation. Call the subclass txtDate. If we change the font color of the parent text box class to purple, the child txtDate also becomes purple, unless we override this behavior by specifying a different font color for txtDate.

Encapsulation

Encapsulation means that the variables (properties) and functions (methods) for accessing the data are grouped together into an object. The object is like a black box and can only be accessed and controlled via its methods and properties. This means that the object is independent of an external state or external objects.

Containership

Containership means that an object can contain another object. For instance, a form can contain a variety of objects, including text boxes. In this case, the form is the parent object of the text box and can be referred to as THIS.PARENT from within a method of the text box. A parent object is not the same as a parent class. The parent class of the text box would be the class from which the text box class inherits its properties and methods.

Delegation

Delegation means passing responsibility from one object to another. For instance, a form object can call a business object to save data. The business object may then delegate the responsibility for actually writing the data into a table to a data object.

Polymorphism

Polymorphism means that different objects can be used in similar ways without regard for their implementation. For example, we might include a Save() method in every data class. That method can be called for any data object, although it may have very different code in each object's method.

Class libraries

Classes are stored in class libraries, and we may organize them as we please. We might have enterprise-level class libraries and then a project-specific library, or in a large project we may have libraries of forms or buttons. Alternatively, we may want to organize our libraries according to the program module where they are used. A third way to organize classes is by the tier of the project they belong with. Because a class may belong to only one library, we might want to have all of the classes used in a COM object, and only those classes, in their own library. We should plan our libraries with the considerations of performance, maintainability, extensibility, and availability as noted earlier. What will happen when the project grows? Are we better off keeping track of many small class libraries or a few larger ones that contain classes we don't need for our project?

Designing an interface for data access

At this point, we can begin to transform the data objects discovered in the logical design into Visual FoxPro code. This is particularly simple because of Visual FoxPro's good object-oriented (OOP) implementation. For instance, we know that we need a data-handling object that we'll call CustomerData, and we want it to be able to access our customer's record and return his name, age, and credit rating. We'll use our MySession class as a parent so our CustomerData class will inherit the DELETED, EXCLUSIVE and CENTURY settings that we've set up to use everywhere in our application. We can translate our need for this class into:

```
DEFINE CLASS CustomerData AS MySession
  Name = ""
  Age = 0
  CreditRating = ""
  PROCEDURE GetCust()
    PARAMETER lpCustId
    USE Customer
    SELECT * FROM Customer WHERE Id = lpCustId INTO CURSOR cCust
    IF _TALLY = 1
      WITH THIS
        .Name = cCust.Name
        .Age = cCust.Age
        .CreditRating = ;
          IIF(yBalanceOwed = 0 OR dLastPayment >= DATE() - 30 ;
          "Good credit", "Bad credit")
      ENDWITH
    ENDIF
    USE IN cCust
    USE IN Customer
  ENDPROC
ENDDEFINE
```

The data object accesses the data entities defined in the logical data model. Using data objects shields the rest of the application from changes in the physical data. For example, if the application switches from using VFP tables to using SQL Server tables, only the data objects need to be changed. The middle tier still asks the CustomerData object to get Name, Age, and CreditRating from our data store in exactly the same way.

Designing the properties and methods of components

Components in the middle tier or business tier are designed in the same way as the data tier, except that these components do not access data directly. Instead, they call on the data components. The business tier enforces business rules. For example, consider a business rule that no patient who's 18 or older can be admitted to the children's unit. Here's an implementation of this rule as part of the HospitalUnit business class:

```
DEFINE CLASS HospitalUnit AS MySession
  PROCEDURE AdmitPatient()
    PARAMETER pnPatientId, pnHospitalUnitId
    IF oUnitInfo.GetName(pnHospitalUnitId) = "Childrens"
      IF .NOT. oPatientData.IsPediatric(pnPatientId)
        RETURN .F.    && Can't admit patient
      ENDIF
    ENDIF
    *!* Business rules satisfied, admit patient using data tier object
    oUnitInfo.AddPatient(pnHospitalUnitId, pnPatientId)
  ENDPROC
ENDDEFINE
```

Using a business tier allows the user interface tier and the data tier to be sheltered from changes in the business rules. This makes the system easier to maintain because the programmer only needs to modify this one class if there are changes to those business rules.

In the preceding example, if the rules for admitting patients change, only the HospitalUnit class must be modified.

Designing the presentation tier

The user interface or presentation tier allows the user to interact with the application. The user will want to be able to access data, so the user interface layer will need to interact with the data components. More importantly for us here, the user will want to be able to enter data, and may not want to have to enter a whole record before discovering that one item is incorrect.

The first thing we think of is to add code in the Valid or LostFocus of our text box or other control to check for something like an improbable date. Unfortunately, if this code is in one of the form's methods, we'll have some difficulty when we decide to move to a new platform for our forms, such as a browser. If the code is in a COM component, we only need code to call the DateCheck() method of the FieldLevelValidator component in the browser, just as we called it from the Visual FoxPro form.

Another advantage to moving the date check out of the form and into a component is that at some point we may have both a form interface and a browser interface in our system. Imagine that our date criteria change. If the code for this were still in the form itself, we would need to change the code in both the form and the browser interfaces. If we wisely design our application with code like this in a component, the call to DateCheck() won't change at all, and we have only to modify one component, retest and redeploy that component, and we are back in business.

We will discuss the creation of the user interface further in Chapter 5, "Creating User Services."

Sample Questions

An application in a Visual FoxPro .EXE is deployed on client machines along with a COM component that does the data validation. The data, in Visual FoxPro tables, reside in the MyData directory of the file server. How many physical tiers is this?

    A. One, because all of the parts are built using the same platform, Visual FoxPro

    B. Two—the client machine and the file server

    C. At least three—the .EXE where the presentation layer resides, the COM component handling the data validation, and the data tier, housed in Visual FoxPro tables

    D. One, because there is one .EXE

Answer: C

The data in the prior example is moved to an Oracle database on a different server. How many physical tiers are there now?

    A. Two, Microsoft, and Oracle

    B. Two, Visual FoxPro and Oracle

    C. Exactly the same as before—changing the physical structure of a tier does not change the number of tiers in the architecture

Answer: C

Further reading

- *Advanced Object Oriented Programming with Visual FoxPro 6.0*, Markus Egger

- "Building Middle Tier Objects in Visual FoxPro," Jim Booth, **http://jamesbooth.com/n-tier.htm**

- *Effective Techniques for Application Development with Visual FoxPro 6.0*, Jim Booth and Steve Sawyer

- *Visual Basic 6 Distributed Exam Cram*, Michael Lane Thomas and Dan Fox, Chapter 2, "Distributed Application Design"

Chapter 4
Establishing the
Development Environment

Configuring the Visual FoxPro development environment is a means for the developer to control the way Visual FoxPro behaves and the way it looks. There is opportunity for "permanent" configuration via Registry settings and "temporary" configuration via SET commands, configuration files, resources files, and command line switches. These configuration settings affect speed, the way comparisons are made, the locations of temporary files, and developer efficiency through the way text is colored on the screen.

In addition to the Visual FoxPro development environment, the developer can configure Visual SourceSafe, Microsoft Transaction Server, Microsoft Internet Information Server, and Microsoft Message Queue Server. Evan loves this paragraph from Whil Hentzen's *The Fundamentals: Building Visual Studio Applications on a Visual FoxPro 6.0 Foundation*:

> *"It never ceases to amaze me to walk into a development shop and see how the developers work. The most mind-numbing experience is to watch a developer start up Visual FoxPro, and then issue three or four attempts of the CD <current app dev directory> command as his first step—because VFP's default location is still set somewhere deep in the bowels of Program Files. Think of all the time you spend building applications to make other people more productive. Doesn't it make sense to tune your own work environment?" (Page 441.)*

Installing Visual FoxPro

There are several options that can be included when installing Visual FoxPro. Here are some noteworthy ones you may want to include during installation:

- Data Access Components—includes ADO, RDS, RDO, OLE DB, ODBC, and Jet drivers and providers

- Additional ActiveX controls

- Enterprise Tools—things such as Visual Studio Analyzer, Visual Modeler, and more

Configuring Visual FoxPro

The Visual FoxPro Integrated Development Environment (IDE) is configurable through the Registry, SET commands, configuration files, resource files, and command line switches. Developers can customize the toolbars and editor as well. We'll be looking at how each of these enhances developer productivity, and the tradeoffs their use involves.

Registry configurations

The Registry is a database of settings that Windows and Windows applications use. Upon starting, Visual FoxPro checks the Registry and sets a number of items based on the values stored in the Registry. **Figure 1** shows the Registry values for VFP6 on Evan's Windows 98 machine. If you use a different version of Windows, the path may be different.

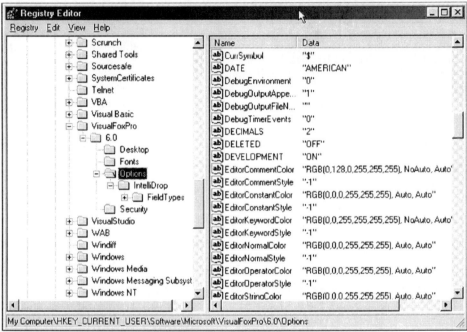

Figure 1. *Visual FoxPro 6 environment settings in the Windows Registry.*

> You can examine your own Registry settings by running RegEdit on Windows 9x, or RegEdit32 on Windows NT4 or Windows 2000. Be careful—making incorrect changes to the Registry can cause serious problems with your computer.

> A developer can make an application programmatically read and write from the Registry, but VFP applications don't do this automatically when run outside of the Visual FoxPro IDE. Registry.PRG in the MSDN sample directory gives an example of how to do this.

Fortunately you don't have to edit the Registry directly to change the VFP environment. Instead, select Tools | Options within VFP to get to the Options screen (see **Figure 2**).

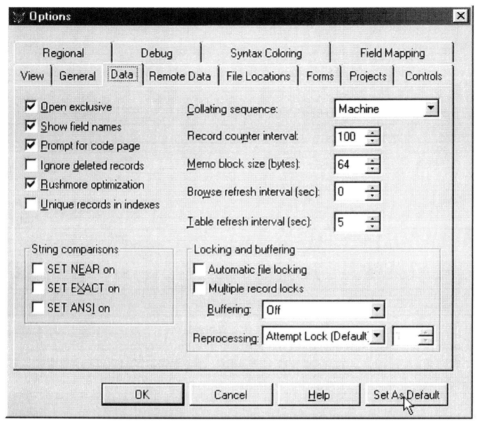

Figure 2. *The Options screen showing settings that are stored in the Registry.*

Here are some of the settings that Cindy and Evan find particularly useful. When using the GUI interface, a check sets the value to ON.

- General | SET DEVELOPMENT—Set to OFF for maximum performance unless you are using an external editor. (SET DEVELOPMENT OFF)

- General | Strict Date Level—Set the value to 2, so VFP will warn you if you are using date constants and functions in a way that could cause year 2000 problems. (SET STRICTDATE TO 2)

- General | Dbase compatibility—Set to OFF. See the VFP Help for the list of affected commands. (SET COMPATIBLE OFF)

- Data | Open exclusive—Many developers find it preferable to have the VFP IDE start with this value set to ON so that they can modify table structures without having to specify the Exclusive option each time. In addition, the developer is usually working with test data that is not shared with others. (SET EXCLUSIVE ON)

- Data | Prompt for code page—Set this to OFF to avoid being prompted for the code page when using an older format FoxPro table. (SET CPDIALOG OFF)

- Data | Rushmore optimization—Set to ON to allow optimization of table commands that uses indexes. Consult the VFP Help file for reasons for setting this to OFF. (SET OPTIMIZE ON)

- Data | Unique records in indexes—Set to OFF. If ON, then only the first of records with duplicate key values are used in indexing. Since VFP doesn't maintain such indexes properly, they should be avoided at all costs. (SET UNIQUE OFF)

- Data | SET NEAR on—Set to ON. The record pointer is moved to the closest match if a SEEK or FIND matches no records. (SET NEAR ON)

- Data | SET EXACT on—Set to OFF. If ON, strings compared must match character for character; the shorter expression is padded on the right with blanks. If OFF, strings are compared character for character until the end of the rightmost expression is reached. Affects Xbase commands. (SET EXACT OFF)

- Data | SET ANSI on—Set to OFF. When ON, shorter strings are padded with blanks; if OFF, strings are compared character by character until the end of the shorter string. Affects SQL commands. (SET ANSI OFF)

- Data | Collating sequence—Set to Machine. General provides case-insensitive sorting for English language text. The other sequences provide ordering specific to those particular languages. In many cases, code page isn't sufficient because there are complex rules for sorting. The key reason to set collate to Machine is that there are negative optimization consequences to using other sequences and, in some cases, you won't find all the data you expect to. (SET COLLATE TO "MACHINE")

- Data | Automatic file locking—Set to ON. When ON, a file is locked when it is edited; if OFF, you need to manually place a lock on a file or record using the Lock command. (SET LOCK ON)

- Data | Multiple Record Locks—Set to ON. When ON, more than one record can be locked at a time. (SET MULTILOCKS ON)

- Data | Buffering—For development, set to OFF.

- Forms | Maximum design area—Set according to the expected size of your users' screens.

- Regional | Century—Set to ON to display all four digits for the year. Use the ROLLOVER keyword of the SET CENTURY command as appropriate within an application. (SET CENTURY ON)

- Regional | Use System Settings—Set to ON to use the settings as configured in the Windows Control Panel. (SET SYSFORMATS ON)

- Controls | Selected—Add controls here that you want to be available from the View Classes button on the Form Controls toolbar.

The options in the Debug and Syntax Coloring tabs are discussed in Chapter 9, "Testing and Debugging the Solution." After making your changes, click the Set As Default button to save the changes into the Registry; otherwise, the changes apply to the current VFP session only. Holding the Shift key while saving echoes the settings to the Command window; they can be copied from there for use in a configuration file or the beginning of an application's Main program, as we discuss in the next section.

SET commands and configuration files

SET commands, such as SET CENTURY ON, offer a means of configuring Visual FoxPro in a temporary manner. These commands can be loaded on startup with a configuration file (Config.FPW), added to the beginning of a program, or typed in the Command window. Each application that you create can have its own Config.FPW file, which can be included in the project or excluded but kept in the project directory, where FoxPro will find it by default. Excluding the file allows changes to be made to the behavior of the application without a rebuild. Think carefully about whether this file should be changeable by the users.

The settings in the configuration file override the Registry settings.

The configuration file does not have to be named Config.FPW. Instead, you can use the -C option at VFP startup to specify any text file. For example:

```
VFP6.EXE -CG:\AnApp.Con
```

VFP applications that are run outside of the VFP IDE don't use the Registry settings when the application loads. Instead, the application uses the settings from the Config.FPW or settings assigned in the application itself.

The configuration file in the current working directory is used. If there isn't one, the one in VFP's home directory is used; otherwise, the DOS path is searched. To determine which Config file is in use, type ? SYS(2019) *in the* Command window.

A configuration file can contain four types of settings. First, it can contain a modified version of the SET commands. For instance, SET CLOCK ON becomes CLOCK = ON. System variables can be set as well. Another powerful feature is that you can execute a module using COMMAND = SuperFramework.APP (as the last line) or by using _STARTUP = SuperFramework.APP anywhere.

For fun (or efficiency!), the configuration file's COMMAND can call a program that customizes the development environment in ways that are not available through SET commands. Here's what Cindy uses in hers when she has enough resources for the added color and graphics:

```
_SCREEN.BACKCOLOR = RGB(204, 157, 230)

_SCREEN.ADDOBJECT("MyPicture", "Image")
```

```
_SCREEN.MyPic.PICTURE = "D:\MyFavoritePicture.BMP"
_SCREEN.MyPic.TOP = 150
_SCREEN.MyPic.LEFT = 300
_SCREEN.MyPic.VISIBLE = .T.

*!* Setup Hacker's guide
DEFINE BAR 10 OF _MSYSTEM KEY ALT+F1 PROMPT "Hacker's Guide"
ON SELECTION BAR 10 OF _MSYSTEM RUN /N3 hh.EXE D:\HackFox.CHM

SET

CD D:\VFPWorkDirectory\
ACTIVATE WINDOW "Trace"
ACTIVATE WINDOW "Watch"
ACTIVATE WINDOW "Locals"
ACTIVATE WINDOW "Call Stack"
ACTIVATE WINDOW "Command"
```

Resource files

When you quit VFP, some of the settings are stored in FoxUser.DBF. The settings stored there include the Command window size and location, which toolbars are currently displayed, and, as the VFP Help says, "more." One common use for the FoxUser.DBF file in an application is to provide the user a customized Print Preview toolbar with the Print button removed.

Command line switches

Command line switches let you further control the VFP IDE and applications that you deploy. **Table 1** shows a list of the switches and their uses.

Table 1. *Switches and their uses.*

Switch	Result
-A	Prevents the Registry and configuration file settings from being used
-B<path/file>	Displays a bitmap as a splash screen
-C<path/file>	Specifies a configuration file to be used
-D<path/file>	Specifies a run-time DLL file to be used
-L<path/file>	Specifies the resource file to be used
-R	Writes the current VFP configuration to the Registry
-T	Prevents the VFP splash screen from being displayed at startup (also /NOLOGO)

To customize the development environment on a per-project basis, use a separate desktop shortcut for each project, and include a command line reference to the configuration file you want to use. One danger of using command line switches in an application is that if the user clicks on the executable directly in Windows Explorer, the expected settings won't be used. For that reason, Evan prefers to use a Config.FPW file.

Toolbars

You can access the toolbar editor by choosing View | Toolbars from the menu. This option lets you specify which toolbars are displayed, create new toolbars, delete toolbars, and reset toolbars to their original state. Toolbar information is stored in the resource file, so you'll want to be sure you have SET RESOURCE ON.

You may want to customize the buttons on one of the system toolbars and save your customized settings in a special resource file. An example is to remove the Print button from the Print Preview toolbar. To do this:

1.   Make a copy of a FoxUser.DBF and FoxUser.FPT, and name them MyResource.DBF and MyResource.FPT.

2.   USE MyResource, ZAP the records, and close the file.

3.   SET RESOURCE TO MyResource

4.   From View | Toolbars, check the Print Preview toolbar, and choose the Customize button.

5.   Add or delete toolbar buttons. In this case, remove the Printer button from the toolbar by dragging it back to the Customize dialog.

6.   SET RESOURCE TO FoxUser.DBF to restore your regular resource file.

7.   Include the MyResource.DBF in the application.

8.   In the application, just before previewing the report, set the resource to MyResource.DBF, and reset to the usual resource file after printing.

Configuring Visual SourceSafe

Microsoft Visual SourceSafe (VSS) is a natural choice for source code control for the Visual FoxPro developer. VSS is included with Visual Studio Enterprise, MSDN Universal, and is also available for purchase as a separate product. VSS provides source code control by allowing developers to check in and check out components, preventing changes from being overwritten. In addition, VSS keeps track of changes to components by using "reverse delta." This means that the changes to a component are stored in a database, allowing changes to be undone easily.

Even lone developers can find benefits in using VSS. For instance, if you have done something horribly wrong to a form and it stops working, you can view the history of changes and roll back to a previous version that is known to work, using the Reverse Delta technology. This is much easier than restoring the file from a backup tape and trying to remember the changes you've made since the backup. Also, if you've added meaningful comments when you check in and check out the modules, VisualSourceSafe uses them to build a database of changes that you have made to a project or module This is perfect for reporting progress to a supervisor or client or showing how you've spent your time.

To install Visual SourceSafe, you need to perform both a client and server installation. The server procedure installs the data folders and utility software onto a file server. Follow this with a client install on each workstation that will access the central repository on the file server. A solo developer can do a client-only install of Visual SourceSafe if he doesn't have access to a file server.

To configure the VFP IDE to work easily with VSS, set it as the default source control provider. Choose Tools | Options, and then click the Projects tab to access this option, as shown in **Figure 3**. From this dialog, you can access other settings that make working with VSS seamless from Visual FoxPro.

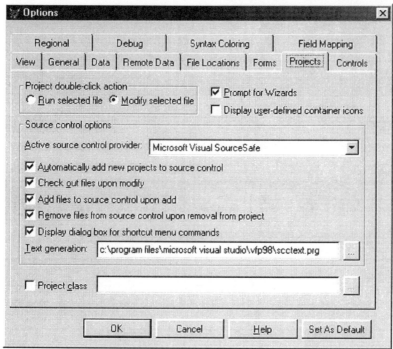

Figure 3. Recommended source control options for use with Visual FoxPro.

The most obvious differences you will notice in the VFP IDE when using the options chosen in Figure 3 are:

- You're asked to log into VSS when opening the first project of a session.

- Each component is marked as checked in (a lock) or checked out (a check mark) in the Project Manager.

- You're asked whether you want to add a new project to VSS each time you create one.

- You're asked whether you want to add or remove components from VSS when you add or remove components from a project.

- You're asked whether you want to check a component out of VSS when you open a component to edit it.

- The Project Manager will have new options to Check In, Check Out, Get The Latest Version, See The History, and History Of Changes added to the context menu of each component.

"Hacker's Guide" recommends running the Visual SourceSafe analyze tool once per week to prevent corruption of the data store.

Accessing Visual SourceSafe via dial-up is reportedly slow. SourceGear offers two useful products, Source*OffSite* and Source*Surf*, that allow Visual SourceSafe files to be shared, and changes tracked, via the Internet. Using these products, developers in different parts of the world can collaborate efficiently instead of relying on e-mail or FTP to share files.

Because some of the file types in a VFP project are binary (most notably forms and reports) and not text, VFP must make text equivalents of the files to track the changes. To specify the file conversion utility within the VFP IDE, select Tools | Options | Projects, and then fill in the Text Generation box with the utility path and name. The default conversion utility is SccText.PRG in the VFP home directory.

Configuring Microsoft Transaction Server

Microsoft Transaction Server (MTS) is a run-time environment for COM components that allows "caching" of components to improve performance. If a component is already loaded in memory, MTS can reuse the component instead of loading another instance from disk. As well, MTS allows for cross-database (SQL and Oracle) database transactions.

To install it, download and run Windows NT 4 Option Pack from **www.microsoft.com/ ntworkstation/downloads/Recommended/ServicePacks/NT4OptPk/Default.asp**. Despite the name, this option pack also works for Windows 95 and 98. Windows 2000 includes MTS. That is about it. There's nothing complicated about installing MTS.

Configuring Microsoft Internet Information Server

Microsoft Internet Information Server (IIS) is a Web server that's included in the Windows NT 4 Option Pack. On Windows 95 and 98, Personal Web Server (PWS) is installed instead of IIS. Just like a Novell file server serves files, IIS serves Web content. Web requests can be made using File Transfer Protocol (FTP) or Hyper Text Transfer Protocol (HTTP). When a user types a URL (Web address) into his browser, the user's computer sends an HTTP request to the Web server. The server responds by sending an HTML character string (plus binary data such as images) back to the user's browser to be displayed. Using a Web server and an HTML front end allows us to make our applications accessible to a wider audience.

Be sure you include Microsoft Management Console (MMC) when installing IIS, since it is not included by default. Microsoft Management Console provides administration for IIS. To start MMC, select Run from the Start menu. In *Internet Applications with Visual FoxPro 6.0*, Rick Strahl suggests some performance-improving configuration options that you may want consider:

- Decrease the number of connections allowed from 10,000 to prevent the Web server from accepting more requests than can be served.

- Reduce the connection timeout value from 900 seconds.

- Turn off ASP sessions if you don't use them.

- Turn on page buffering.

- Limit threads to no more than 50 per processor.

Configuring Microsoft Message Queue

Microsoft Message Queue Server (MSMQ) provides a method for applications to send, receive, and store messages. One can simplistically think of this as e-mail for applications. It requires SQL Server 6.5 or higher. As with MTS and IIS, it is included in the Windows NT 4 Option Pack.

Why would you want to use MSMQ? If you think of a conventional COM application, all processing and communication happens in real time. For example, a user requests product info via a browser on a Web site. The ASP script on the Web server calls a COM component, which requests data from SQL Server. Each part of the application calls another component and returns a response to the customer within a split second. However, there are times when an immediate response is unnecessary, or a system component can't process or communicate in real time. In those situations, we need a way of storing transactions if a part of the system goes down, or if it is too expensive to communicate in real time and we need to guarantee delivery of messages. Bob Tracey of Driftwood, Texas tipped us off to a unique use of this technology: mobile computing. The client notebook computer queues messages while disconnected and then sends the messages once connected to the network again.

An example of a time when an immediate response is not needed is when a customer buys an item on the Web. It's not necessary to wait several minutes online for a credit card transaction to be approved because this is easily done while the order is waiting to be packaged. If there is a problem approving the transaction, the Web server can send an e-mail to the customer, or it can try to approve the transaction again the next business day. This is different from the needs of a retail store where the customer expects to walk out the door with the product in his hand.

Stability and reliability are two of the big reasons for implementing MSMQ, but performance is another. If requests to the server are queued, system load can be controled. Instead of having lulls in traffic then spikes that can affect the response time of other components, the queued components are served at a predictable rate.

To install MSMQ, you need to configure a Windows NT or Windows 2000 server running SQL Server 6.5 or higher as the Primary Enterprise Controller (PEC). The PEC is the first part of an MSMQ environment that must be installed. Each site then has a Primary Site Controller (PSC). For single-site systems, the PEC and PSC can be the same computer. Next are two types of client installs: Independent and Dependent. Independent clients queue only locally and operate without a PEC. Dependent clients must be connected to a PEC (or a Backup Site Controller). In addition, there can be a Backup Site Controller that maintains a backup of the MSMQ configuration database, but this is not required for MSMQ to work.

Sample Questions

Why would a lone developer find Visual SourceSafe useful? (Choose all that apply.)

A. Other developers may join the project someday.

B. It provides the ability to undo changes to source files.

C. It has nothing to offer the lone developer.

D. It makes opening project files faster.

E. It provides an extra backup of crucial files.

Answer: B and E

To configure Visual SourceSafe to be used by a group of developers, you must:

A. Perform a client install on each workstation.

B. Perform a server install on a departmental server.

C. Perform a server install on a departmental server, then a client install on each workstation.

D. Nothing; Visual SourceSafe is built into Windows.

Answer: C

Further reading

- *1001 Things You Wanted to Know About Visual FoxPro*, Marcia Akins, Andy Kramek and Rick Schummer, Chapter 1, "Controlling the VFP Environment"

- "Building Large Scale Web Applications with Visual FoxPro," Rick Strahl, **www.west-wind.com/presentations/largeweb/default.htm**

- *Essential SourceSafe*, Ted Roche, Chapter 1, "SourceSafe Installation"

- *The Fundamentals: Building Visual Studio Applications on a Visual FoxPro Foundation*, Whil Hentzen, Section 4, "The Development Environment"

- *Hacker's Guide to Visual FoxPro 6.0*, Tamar Granor and Ted Roche, "A Source is a Source, Of Course, Of Course"

- *Internet Applications with Visual FoxPro 6.0*, Rick Strahl, Chapter 3, "Setting Up"

- "Microsoft Message Queuing," **www.microsoft.com/msmq/**

- "Microsoft Transaction Server for Visual FoxPro Developers," Randy Brown, Microsoft Corporation, **http://msdn.microsoft.com/library/techart/MTSVFP.htm**

- *Microsoft Visual FoxPro 6.0 Programmer's Guide*, Chapter 29, "Developing in Teams"

- **http://fox.wikis.com/wc.dll?Wiki~SettingUpMTS**

- "Using Microsoft Transaction Server with VFP," Rick Strahl, **www.west-wind.com/presentations/mts/mts.htm**

- "Using MSMQ with Microsoft Visual FoxPro 6.0," Randy Brown, Microsoft Corporation, **http://msdn.microsoft.com/library/default.asp?URL=/ library/techart/msmqwvfp6.htm**

- *Visual FoxPro Installation Guide*, Chapter 3, "Configuring Visual FoxPro"

- **www.microsoft.com/ntworkstation/downloads/Recommended/ServicePacks/ NT4OptPk/Default.asp**

- "Using SourceSafe Boost Efficiently," EPS Software, **www.eps-software.com/isapi/eps.dll?KnowledgeBase~DisplayKBDocument~16**

- *Visual Basic 6 Distributed Exam Cram*, Chapter 3, "Configuring a Development Environment"

Third-party software

- Markus Egger's SourceSafe Boost 1.0, .APP without source code, Freeware, **www.eps-software.com/isapi/eps.dll?products~ga+SourceSafe+Boost+1.0**

- Source*OffSite,* an Internet access solution for using Microsoft Visual SourceSafe for remote developers, **www.sourcegear.com/SOS** (see Web site for pricing)

- Source*Surf*, a read-only reporting tool that allows your entire team to view changes and track usage of its SourceSafe database from any Web browser, **www.sourcegear.com/SRF** (see Web site for pricing)

Chapter 5
Creating User Services

User services are the clothes our data wears when facing the outside world. Cindy remembers a presentation of Open Software Solutions' award-winning 911-call center software where the developer, Alan Biddle, remarked that his users spent all day using his software to do a mission-critical job, and that one of his goals in designing it was that it should be friendly and easy to use. We can either present an interface that is ugly, awkward, and unintuitive, or one that is easy to look at, intuitive to use, and forgiving when we err. In addition, we want our application to be usable even by those with functional limitations such as poor hearing or vision.

Microsoft's document "Application Specification for Microsoft Windows 2000 for Desktop Applications" is a guide for creating applications that are manageable, reliable, and reduce the cost of ownership, both for the developer and the customer. Conformance to these specifications is a requirement for applications wanting the Microsoft "Certified for Microsoft Windows" logo. The specifications support compliance with the Americans with Disabilities Act and similar legislation worldwide, roaming users and multiple users on one machine, simplified machine replacement, security, and migration to an upgraded operating system. Many developers will not be able to invest in full compliance with the specification, but we should all be familiar with the guidelines and know why we're departing from them if we need or choose to do so.

If we offer the user a logical, predictable interface where she can be productive without a lot of specialized training, isn't frustrated when entering incorrect data, and can easily get a hint when she needs one, we'll have done our job. When our application compiles data and produces reports, they should be pleasing to the eye and understandable at face value. Finally, the user services layer of the application should also be our first defense against errors and a major contributor to our debugging strategy, offering the user a good explanation, and saving vital information for us, should an error occur.

Providing a personalized interface

Among the requirements for Windows Certification, Microsoft requires that an application support the following:

- Standard system size, color, font, and input settings

- Compatibility with the High Contrast option

- Documented keyboard access to all features

- Notification of keyboard focus location

- No reliance on sound as the only way to notify the user of an event

While we may not always be required to support all of these features, we should understand that the goal for all of them is to assist the user, especially one who is less able, to use the software, and to provide a more pleasant and efficient experience. User-customizable fonts, sizes, and input settings prevent problems that might stem from a user with blue-green color blindness not being able to distinguish blue text on a green background, for example. The High Contrast option improves readability, and the keyboard focus allows a user to follow the action of a screen when using the Magnifier accessory that comes with Windows 98 and Windows 2000. Although Windows offers a blinking desktop in addition to the usual "beep" that accompanies an error, we should consider giving even the user without disabilities visual notifications of such things as errors. Through means such as message boxes, we avoid problems for users who can't hear the "beep," either because of hearing loss, because they're in a noisy environment, or because their .MP3 is playing.

Personalizing colors

One of the simplest ways to comply with these guidelines, and to keep the users happy, is to use the default Windows colors everywhere in your application. If the customer wants company colors to be used, suggest that they appear on a splash screen, or as a logo or border, not for the whole screen space. The user with disabilities will be able to do his job, and the user with no disabilities will be pleased to have his favorite color or font available.

Although there are a number of customizable settings in Appearance, they don't affect text such as that found in an Edit box. A perfect way to customize this is by using a configuration file, or storing settings in the Windows Registry. Care should be taken to determine whether the customizations should follow the user from machine to machine, as those saved in the Registry will not, while those saved in a configuration file on the network could provide this capability.

All Visual FoxPro controls use the Windows colors by default, but the terminology associated with colors is confusing. The ColorSource property determines how the colors are set. Choosing option 4, Windows Control Panel (3D Colors), means that the object takes its colors from those set for dialog boxes in the Control Panel, while choosing 5 for ColorSource uses document, rather than dialog, colors. Setting any of the object's color settings overrides the ColorSource settings for that object.

Keyboard and mouse access

Ever "lost" your mouse pointer when Windows is showing signs of needing a reboot? If you have, you may remember whether you knew enough keyboard navigation commands at the time to move about the keyboard and close up shop cleanly before you rebooted. Whether or not you've had that experience, perhaps you can remember the awkward feeling of using a touch pad for the first time. Alternatively, do you read e-mail over morning coffee, using the mouse to navigate, and reluctantly have to set the mug down to type an answer?

As you design the user interface, be careful to offer a choice at all times as to how to reach each control on the form. Focus should move logically according to the expected workflow, from the first control to the last. Offer hot keys, signified by the underlined letter in the caption and accessed in combination with the Alt key, and keyboard shortcuts, usually shown in menus to the right of the item and accessed in combination with the Ctrl key, for mouse-less input. In some cases, you may need to consider options for mouse-only input, such as an onscreen keyboard. Generally, someone who needs that capability will have a utility for it, and the application just needs to accept that data, but you will need to accommodate the screen space that might be occupied by the utility.

Sound and focus

Many of us are used to our computers beeping at us when there is an error. We've never considered that a user might not hear it, and we've never toyed with the accessibility options in the Control Panel. The accessibility options offer a flashing window or desktop when a sound occurs. The Windows Logo requirements don't require additional notification for a sound that accompanies information, like one that might accompany a message box, because the message box itself offers enough notification.

Exposing the location of the keyboard focus allows a magnifier to move about the window automatically as the focus changes from one control to the next. Using the Windows API CreateCaret function to create an invisible caret and move it about does this. The magnifier will follow this caret automatically.

User or group options

Often we are asked to provide options in our applications that should only be available to one user or a small group of users. This is often requested for specialized processes such as approving timecards, purchase orders over a certain amount, or invoice payments.

At the opening of the application, you can ask the user to identify himself and extract from the Security table information such as belonging to a particular hierarchical group or his security level. Following that, you can easily enable or disable form features based on the user's security level.

For timecard approval, you can fetch records to approve based on which employees the user supervises, again by looking in a table. For other role-based security, you can pass all requests for data through a business object that asks, "Who wants to know?" before recording that the data was requested and passing back values or records.

Planning the interface

In *Microsoft Windows User Experience,* Microsoft lays out guidelines for interface planning, to promote "good interface design and visual and functional consistency." Visual and functional consistency makes it easy for the users to move efficiently through their work with a minimum of training, because they know what to expect and how to use the different controls. Hot keys are an example. Cindy remembers the first time she realized what the underline marks meant in the text beside form controls. Now she's sure to add them everywhere in her interfaces because she finds keyboard-only entry more efficient.

The tools available to us for interacting with the user include:

- Form

- Menu and shortcut menu

- Toolbar

- Text box

- Edit box

- Command button

- Command group

- Option group

- Check box

- Combo box

- List box

- Spinner

- Grid

- Page frame

For a complete discussion of these controls, see Part 3 of the *Microsoft Visual FoxPro 6.0 Programmer's Guide*. We'll touch on some key points here.

Forms

Forms can be made to behave in different ways using a combination of the MDIForm, ShowWindow, and WindowType properties. Use MDIForm to determine whether a child form should be united with its parent form when maximized, use ShowWindow to determine whether the form is independent of the main VFP window, and use WindowType to determine whether the user may interact with other forms while this one is open.

Visual FoxPro forms, formsets, toolbars, and reports all include a data environment and a data session that we can use to make the data housekeeping chores easier. We'll discuss data environment and data session in turn.

Data environment

The data environment of a form is a subclass of the Visual FoxPro DataEnvironment base class, and we can access it through the GUI Data Environment designer. The objects in the data environment are cursors and relations, both subclasses of the Visual FoxPro Cursor and Relation classes. Add tables and views to the data environment by right-clicking the form, choosing Data Environment…, and then right-clicking the Data Environment and choosing Add… Bring up the method window to add code to any of the data environment's methods by double-clicking the data environment.

The AutoOpenTables and AutoCloseTables properties of the data environment that allow us to automatically open and close all of the cursors in the environment are especially useful. The NoDataOnLoad property of a cursor object allows us to retrieve the structure of the underlying table or view and bind form objects to it as the form loads, without having actual data available such as data retrieved through a parameterized view.

Having cursors in the data environment of a form allows us to drag and drop table fields onto a form where they can become labels and text boxes, or a grid.

Data session

In Visual FoxPro, the current working data environment is called the "data session." There can be more than one data session active at any one time, and each behaves as if it were one instance of a Visual FoxPro session on one computer. As described previously, forms, formsets, and toolbars have data sessions.

A data session can be private or default to the data session that is current when the form is called. When a form defaults to the current data session, it automatically "sees" the tables, relations, and record pointers that are in existence when it opens, and shares them with other forms using that data session. Opening a form with a private data session, on the other hand, is similar in effect to opening that form in a separate instance of Visual FoxPro. The view of the tables, relations, and record pointers seen by a form with a private data session is not seen by other forms, excepting any child forms that are set to use the "default" data session, which, in this case, is actually the private data session of the parent form.

Consider the situation where the user is entering a new customer's information and the telephone rings with an existing customer who wants to change his fax number in the database. The existing customer doesn't want to be put on hold while the user finishes the current edits, and the user doesn't want an unanticipated TABLEUPDATE() to occur on her unfinished edits because the record pointer moved while she was trying to enter the information relayed over the telephone. If the Customer Information form has a private data session, the user can easily open an additional instance of it and complete the fax number change without disturbing the record pointer of the unfinished edits on the previous instance of the form.

Settings that affect the way the application interacts with data, such as CENTURY, EXACT, and DELETED, are scoped to the data session, so you may want to build your usual settings for these into the Load() of your base form class, and use that class as the parent for all forms in your application. For COM objects where the bulk of a form class is unnecessary and unwanted, a lightweight Session class with no user interface was added to Visual FoxPro in Service Pack 3.

Menu systems

To aid the user in navigating our system, Visual FoxPro gives us the ability to use menus, the bars across the top of our applications with the File, Edit, and Help choices; and shortcut or context menus, the lists of choices brought up by right-clicking on an object. For ease of use, menu items should be grouped logically with spacers between them, and have a combination of access or hot keys, and keyboard shortcuts.

Menus

Use the Visual FoxPro Menu Designer to create menus. To create a menu, use the Other tab of the Project Manager, highlight Menus, and choose New. Since you're creating a menu, choose the Menu button. At this point, you can use the Menu | Quick Menu option to let Visual FoxPro create the skeleton menu for you, or you can create the menu completely by hand. Menus can also be created or modified by typing CREATE MENU or MODIFY MENU in the Command window.

The items listed at the Menu Bar level are displayed across the top of the menu, and the items listed at the Submenu level are the ones that drop down. Precede a letter with "\<" to indicate a hot key; use "\-" by itself in a row to create a spacer or dividing line. Use the button in the Options column to bring up a dialog where you can specify a keyboard shortcut, skip (disable) a menu item under certain conditions, and add a status bar message. Use the Preview button to see what the menu will look like.

You must generate your menu before using it by choosing Menu | Generate; the result is a program file with the .MPR extension. (Building a project performs this step automatically.) To call the menu, use DO `MyMenu.MPR`. This code is most commonly located in the Main program or in a form's Init() method. For more detail on creating menus, see Chapter 11, "Creating Menus and Toolbars," in the *Microsoft Visual FoxPro 6.0 Programmer's Guide*, or look inside an .MPR file to see how it all works.

Shortcut menus

Shortcut, or context menus are the ones that appear when the user clicks the right mouse button, and they provide a nice way to assist the user with context-sensitive help or a list of functions that apply only in that context. To make a shortcut menu, choose New (Menu) in the Project Manager, choose the Shortcut button, and continue creating and generating as described previously. To call the menu, use DO `MyShortcutMenu.MPR` in the RightClick() method of your form or control.

Form controls in general

Form controls such as text boxes, list and combo boxes, option buttons, and command buttons allow the user to make choices, enter data, and perform actions. Choosing the correct control for the job, and arranging controls on the form in a logical manner goes a long way toward making your application easy to use.

Add a control to a form by clicking it on the Form Controls toolbar and then dropping it on the form. To use custom, subclassed controls, click the Books icon (its ToolTip is "View Classes") on the Form Controls toolbar and choose Add. Navigate to the class library that contains your custom controls and choose it. The new class library's controls are added to the toolbar, replacing the Standard ones, and the new class library is added to the list of sources presented by the View Classes button. Switch back and forth from FoxPro base classes to your custom controls using the Books button and the pop-up menu. Other ways to add controls to a form include dragging the controls from a class library in the Project Manager or the Component Gallery, or dragging fields or whole tables from the form's data environment to the form, as mentioned previously in the "Data environment" section. We'll talk more about this last option later on in the "Binding data to controls" section of this chapter.

To change properties of controls, right-click and choose Properties to bring up the Properties window, and edit the property values there. Assign code to a method associated with the control by double-clicking the method on the Methods tab of the Properties window, or just double-clicking on the control itself, choosing the method from the Procedures list, and typing the code in the window.

When adding method code, consider carefully whether you want to execute the inherited code associated with the event and, if so, whether it should be executed before or after your custom code. When adding code to a method, you must specifically call the inherited code with DODEFAULT() or it will not be executed. In contrast, use NODEFAULT in the method code to prevent the built-in base class behavior from occurring when no method code has been added.

Toolbars

A custom toolbar has some similarities to its relative, the form, and plenty of differences. We can create toolbars by subclassing the Toolbar class that comes with Visual FoxPro. A toolbar automatically sizes and shapes itself according to the number of controls it has on it, and where it is located, becoming long when docked at the top or bottom of the screen, narrow and tall when docked at the side, and of varying shapes when in the middle of the screen.

Instantiate the toolbar whenever you need it to be available in your application by using code like the following:

```
SET CLASSLIB TO ClassLibThatHasMyToolbar ADDITIVE
oToolbar = CREATEOBJECT("MyToolbar")
oToolbar.SHOW()
```

Change properties and add code in the methods of the toolbar buttons the same way you do for form buttons.

To coordinate menus and toolbars, create a submenu prompt for each button on the toolbar. In the menu, use the Command choice to call the Click() of the toolbar button, or, even better, have both the menu and the toolbar call a method of the form they act upon. This is easily accomplished by calling a method of _SCREEN.ActiveForm, as in:

```
_SCREEN.ActiveForm.ValidateAndSaveChanges()
```

One of the most important things to remember about toolbars is that they usually cannot receive focus, so if a user goes from a text box on a form to a toolbar button, the text box's LostFocus never fires. The LostFocus can be fired by calling the SetFocus() method code of the current control specifically in the toolbar button's click event with the following, causing the LostFocus event and any associated method code to fire:

```
_SCREEN.ActiveForm.ActiveControl.SetFocus()
```

User interaction with forms

Forms are container objects, and like other containers, they don't do much by themselves, but when they're populated with controls that the user can interact with, they become the presentation layer of our application.

Form use generally falls into two categories: dialog forms that allow the user to make a choice or trigger an action such as a report, and data interaction forms. While a dialog form may ask for some data item like a time period for which report data should be gathered, these items are not usually stored beyond the life of the form. In contrast, a data interaction form is designed to gather data from the user and save it into the application's tables, or present existing data and allow the user to change it.

Whether we've made it obvious to our users or not, our data interaction forms usually have three states: view, add, and edit. In addition, our forms usually provide a way to separate the edits from the live data so that changes can be easily undone. Managing these three states and appropriately buffering and committing edits to the live data consume much of our form coding.

Form properties, events, and methods

Because a form is a container, its properties and methods are a great place to put values or code that need to be available to all objects contained in the form. Form properties are the OOP way to have a form-specific variable available to every method of the form. Add custom properties or methods using the New Property... and New Method... choices on the Form menu.

It's always difficult to conceptualize the difference between events and methods, but an event is something that happens, and a method is the place to put code that runs when that event occurs. You can also create a method that is not specifically associated with an event. Typically, you're better off adding custom methods to forms, or to other controls, and limiting the code in the event method to calls to the custom methods that actually do the work.

Of particular importance are form events that fire when a form is opened or closed, because that is where a lot of our housekeeping will need to be done. When the form opens, these form-level events fire: Load, the data environment's Init and the form's Init, Activate, When, and GotFocus. When it closes, some of these form-level events fire, depending on how it is closed: QueryUnload, Destroy, Unload, and the data environment's Destroy. Notice that the form's Init follows the data environment's Init so all the cursors are open and available to be bound to the form controls as they're created, and that the data environment's Destroy follows the form's final events so you have an opportunity to check for unsaved data changes while the data is still available. There's more about events later in this chapter in the "Processing entered data" section and again in Chapter 9, "Testing and Debugging the Solution."

Binding data to controls

One of the simplest ways to bind data to form controls is to drag the fields or the whole table from the data environment to the form. When you do this, the controls assigned to the fields depend on the field type, and use the classes assigned as specified in Tools | Options | Field Mapping, where you can specify how to replace the Visual FoxPro base classes with your own class libraries. By default, when you drag fields from the data environment, all field types map to text boxes except for memos, which default to edit boxes; general fields, which default to OLE bound controls; and logical fields, which default to check boxes. The field caption (or field name if there is no caption) becomes a label on the form. When groups of fields are dragged and dropped together, the result defaults to a grid control, but you can opt to drop multiple controls instead by holding the right mouse button down as you drag and choosing Create Multiple Controls Here. The Field Mapping settings let you change the classes that are used in this situation.

A few things are worth mentioning when binding data to controls. First, you probably want some safety layer between the user and the actual data, so you may be buffering your data or using a view.

Second, some controls, like check boxes and option groups, can be used with more than one data type, and when bound to data, automatically take the data type of the field they're bound to. If these controls are not bound, such as those used for setting a form property or variable, you can set the Value to an empty value of the desired type in the Properties window.

Third, a form with data bound to a view can take time to load while the view is populated. If the view is parameterized, the user won't usually be able to supply a parameter until the form loads, though you can code a default parameter. Decrease form load time and user frustration by setting the NoDataOnLoad property of the cursors in the form's data environment to .T. so FoxPro can get the structure of the cursor, usually a quick process, and then REQUERY() when you're ready to fetch the data.

ActiveX controls

A variety of ActiveX controls are installed with Visual FoxPro and are freely distributable, including these:

- Microsoft Date and Time Picker Control

- Microsoft Chart Control

- Microsoft ImageList Control

- Microsoft ListView Control

- Microsoft ProgressBar Control

- Microsoft Slider Control

- Microsoft TreeView Control

- Microsoft Rich Textbox Control

- Microsoft Internet Transfer Control

You may also have other ActiveX controls available from Microsoft or other vendors. Check with the vendors for distribution information for these controls.

To add any of these controls to your form, first use the Controls tab of the Options dialog to find and select the controls you want to have available. They will then appear on the ActiveX Controls toolbar, accessed by clicking the Books button ("View Classes" ToolTip) on the Form Controls toolbar and choosing ActiveX Controls from the shortcut menu. Each ActiveX control comes with its own set of properties, events, and methods.

Manipulating controls at run time

Visual FoxPro allows us to add and remove objects to our forms at run time, and to change their properties as well.

Use the AddObject(), NewObject(), and RemoveObject() methods of a container—in this case, a form—to add and remove controls at run time. This means you can add columns to a grid, or buttons to a command group, depending on conditions such as the permissions level of the user. You might put all of the form controls inside a container and save it as a class at design time, and then add the class to the form at run time using code such as:

```
THISFORM.NewObject("HomeAddress", "cntAddress", "MyAddressClasses")
```

An excellent example of the usefulness of adding or changing controls at run time is the case of a form with a page frame control containing several pages full of controls, causing the form instantiation to be slow. The solution to speeding up the instantiation is to instantiate only the controls on the page that will be visible when the form first loads, and instantiate the controls on each hidden page only as the user switches to it.

The ability to change values of properties at run time enables us to highlight the current record in a grid, and enable and disable buttons in a command group. You can use the SetAll() method of the container and, if necessary, IIF() to efficiently set properties of a group of controls.

Using the _SCREEN.ActiveForms collection

_SCREEN is a Visual FoxPro system variable that is available at all times; it contains an object reference to the main Visual FoxPro window. One of its properties is the ActiveForms collection, basically a list of all forms and toolbars that are open. The items in this collection are listed in the order in which they were last activated. Use the _SCREEN.ActiveForms collection as a convenient way to cycle through all open forms and perform an action such as checking to see whether an instance of a particular form is already open, or checking for unfinished edits and closing the form.

Validating user input

Data is validated in the user interface and business tiers to prevent inconsistent or incorrect data being stored in the data tier. The rules or tests that data must pass to be accepted into the data tier are called business rules, and these rules are conditions of the business or environment that the software is modeling. An example of a business rule is "Only patients under 18 years of age can be admitted to the children's unit." In addition to business rules, there are data validation rules, which are rules that aren't related to the business domain, but instead are for data consistency. An example is "Gender cannot be empty."

Evan uses the middle, or business, tier to validate his data even when he creates simple applications. Storing all of the business rules together in the business tier makes changing the application much easier when the business rules change, and validating data in the business tier prevents the need to rewrite the business tier of the application if the user interface changes from a VFP front end to a browser, for example. In addition, the software will be easier to understand when another programmer needs to modify it in the future.

Data can be validated at the field level, record level, table level, and database level, depending on which other values they must be compared against. An example of field-level validation is "Admission date cannot be in the future," and an example of record-level validation is "Discharge cannot be before admission date." An example of table-level validation is "Daily Care cannot be charged more than once for the same date," and finally, an example of database-level validation is "Patient's attending physician must have admitting privileges at this hospital."

Validation can occur on each field in the form as the user leaves it, and also at the record level when the Save button is clicked. Evan thinks that a combination of these two methods works well to avoid user frustration and improve accuracy. There may be situations where you would use one method exclusively over the other. Some customers may require that their users know immediately if they enter an invalid item, and be returned to the entry control so they can correct it, instead of having to tab back to any incorrect fields after a Save button is clicked. As examples of how this might be implemented, **Listing 1** shows the validation code in the

PatientDischarge business rule class, and **Listing 2** shows how the class might be called from a method within a form.

Listing 1. *Validation rules in business objects.*

```
DEFINE CLASS PatientDischarge AS CUSTOM
  cValidMessage = ""

  *!* Validate the field, assume parameters are present and of correct type
  FUNCTION ValidateField
    LPARAMETERS pcFieldName, pData

    THIS.cValidMessage = ""
    DO CASE
     CASE UPPER(pcFieldName) = "ADMITDATE"
        IF pData > DATE()  && Admit date is in future, biz rule violated
          THIS.cValidMessage = "Admit date cannot be in the future"
          RETURN .F.
        ENDIF
        RETURN .T.

      CASE UPPER(pcFieldName) = "DISDATE"
        IF pData > DATE()  && Discharge date is in future, biz rule violated
          THIS.cValidMessage = "Discharge date cannot be in the future"
          RETURN .F.
        ENDIF
        RETURN .T.

      OTHERWISE     && Field not found
        THIS.cValidMessage = "Field not found"
        RETURN .F.
      ENDCASE
  ENDFUNC

  *!* Validate the record
  *!* Assume parameters are present and of the correct type
  FUNCTION ValidateRecord
    LPARAMETERS pnPatientId, pdAdmitDate, pdDisDate

    *!* To make the example simpler, pass the data as parameters
    *!* We could also pass an XML string

    THIS.cValidMessage = ""

    *!* Field validations for this record
    IF ;
      NOT THIS.ValidateField("AdmitDate", pdAdmitDate) ;
      OR ;
      NOT THIS.ValidateField("DisDate", pdDisDate)
      RETURN .F.
    ENDIF

    *!* Record validations comparing fields within the record
    IF pdDisDate < pdAdmitDate     && Discharge date is before Admit date
      THIS.cValidMessage = ;
        "Patient discharge date cannot be before admit date"
      RETURN .F.
```

```
    ENDIF

    *!* Validate with other data outside this table
    *!* by calling a method of an existing Patient object
    *!* which has been instantiated elsewhere
    IF oPatient.DocSignedDisharge(pnPatientId) = .F.
      THIS.cValidMessage = ;
        "Physician has not signed discharge papers, cannot discharge"
    ENDIF
  ENDFUNC
ENDDEF
```

Listing 2. Using the PatientDischarge business object in the Valid event of a text box and in the Click event of the Save button.

```
*!* txtAdmit.Valid()
*!* Validates discharge date using the PatientDischarge object
IF NOT oPatientDischarge.ValidateField("DischargeDate", THIS.VALUE)
  MessageBox(oPatientDischarge.cValidMessage, "Validation")
  RETURN .F.
ENDIF

*!* btnSave.Click()
*!* If data is valid, save
IF oPatAdmit.ValidateRecord(THIS.txtPatId, THIS.txtAdmit, THIS.txtDischarge)
  THISFORM.SaveData()
ELSE
  MessageBox(oPatAdmit.cValidMessage, "Validation")
  RETURN .F.
ENDIF
```

Another validation concern is the handling of lookup tables. The validation process can be more efficient if seldom-changed validation tables such as a list of provinces, states, or counties are downloaded to the client when the application starts up. This prevents a potentially slow round trip to the server to compare entered data to the list of valid choices.

Processing entered data

Let's talk about some of the form and control events and methods that you can use as you process data entered on a form. Form events (and their associated methods) that we'll discuss are: Load, Init, QueryUnload, Release, Refresh, Activate, and Deactivate. We'll also discuss Click, Init, GotFocus, LostFocus, and Valid events and methods for form controls.

Form events and methods

The Load event of a form fires before the form, or any of its contained controls, is created. If we haven't used the form's data environment to automatically open tables, the Load() method is the place where we can prepare and manipulate data such as creating cursors from tables, opening views, and initializing arrays before the data is bound to the controls.

The Init of the form fires after the Init events of all the controls on the form. At this point, you can decide whether you want to continue loading the form, or return .F. from the Init() method and abandon execution of the form. For instance, in the Init() you may check your security object and decide that the user shouldn't be able to see the data presented on the form. Accomplish this by issuing RETURN .F. to cause the form to be destroyed before it goes any further.

QueryUnload and Release are mutually exclusive events when a form is being closed down. QueryUnload is fired whenever the form is closed, except when it is closed by an explicit call to Release(). The methods associated with these two events are a great place to check the data for unsaved changes before letting the form close, but because they are mutually exclusive, the best approach is to add a custom method such as CheckAllBeforeClosing() to the form and call it from both the Release() and QueryUnload() methods. Typical code in a method like CheckAllBeforeClosing() includes asking the user how to handle unsaved changes, if there are any, before continuing on to close the form.

The Activate event of a form fires when the form gets focus after another form has had focus, and also fires when the form's Show() method is called. Similarly, the Deactivate event fires when another form gets focus or when the form's Hide() method is called. You may want to call the Refresh() method to update the visible data on a form each time the Activate event fires.

Form control events and methods

A control's Init() method is the logical place to assign its value, especially if the value is not simply bound to a field in a table. For instance, you might have a text box with the account representative's name on a customer display form, but because the name is from the related AccountReps table, you can't just bind it to the control. You may use code like the following in the Init() method:

```
*!* txtAccountRepName Init()
*!* Find account representative for this customer and show the name
IF !USED("AccountReps")
  USE AccountReps IN 0
ENDIF
THIS.VALUE = ;
  IIF(SEEK(Customer.fkAccountRep, "AccountReps", "AccountRepID"), ;
  AccountReps.AccountRepName, "No account rep")
USE IN AccountReps
```

The GotFocus event fires just before a control receive focus. One good use of the method associated with this event is to fill a combo box with a fresh set of values based on the value of other data, just as the user accesses the combo box.

The LostFocus event fires when the control loses focus, and is a good place to update the status of other controls based on the value of the current control. This example disables the spouse name field if the marital status is "Single."

```
*!* cboMaritalStatus LostFocus()
*!* Enable txtSpouseName when marital status is not Single
THIS.PARENT.txtSpouseName.ENABLED = (UPPER(THIS.VALUE) <> "SINGLE")
```

Not surprisingly, the Valid() method of a control is a good place to validate the data that has been entered in it. If the data isn't valid, returning .F. in the method causes the focus to stay on the control.

The Refresh() method of a control is a good place to determine its status, such as whether or not its value needs to be updated or whether it should be enabled or disabled.

Much of our user interaction depends on the Click events of the controls on our forms, and much of our code is in the Click() methods, or is called from them. The event fires when the user clicks the controls with the mouse or uses a keyboard equivalent.

You may sometimes display calculated values that are based on other data entered on the form. If you have a text box that contains price, and another that contains quantity, and you want to calculate the line item total, you could use code like THIS.PARENT.txtTotal. CalculateTotal() in the LostFocus() method of each of the involved text boxes, and include a call to THIS.PARENT.txtTotal.REFRESH() in the CalculateTotal() method of txtTotal. As another example, suppose you have numerous controls on a form whose Enabled property depends on whether you are adding or editing data. In the Click() of your Add/Edit/Save/Cancel command group, add a call to a method that iterates through all the controls on the form and adjusts their status based on which of the buttons in the group was clicked, and the value of a custom property you have added to each of the form controls for this purpose.

Compiling data in reports

Many times the goal of our application is to collect and record data for management reports. Reports are ambassadors for our software, and often the primary way the customer feels about the value of our application is by the looks and accuracy of the reports we present to him; "visual validation" becomes the name of the game.

Reports should have white space, draw the reader's eye in a logical manner across the page, and tell the reader everything he wants to know. You should make the effort to understand the customer's business needs so you'll know which statistics he'll want to see. If you've shown the order totals and he immediately pulls out the calculator to determine the amount of the average sale, you've missed something.

The best method we've found for creating reports is to select all of the data, exactly the way it should appear on the report, into a cursor or view, and then run the report from that. Leave the report's data environment empty. Refer to the items in the report controls as MyField, rather than MyTable.MyField. We've seen more than our fair share of newsgroup questions from users trying to debug reports run from related tables.

Visual FoxPro stores printer-specific information in the Expr, Tag, and Tag2 fields of the first record of the .FRX table. To avoid printer problems when the customer is using a different type of printer, clear out this information using code like the following before distributing the application:

```
USE MyReport.FRX

*!* Clear Tag and Tag2
BLANK FIELDS Tag, Tag2

*!* In the Expr field,
*!* keep reference to orientation, papersize, copies, color, collate
*!* delete other printer-specific references by preceding with "*"
REPLACE Expr WITH STRTRAN(Expr, "DRIVER", "*DRIVER")
REPLACE Expr WITH STRTRAN(Expr, "DEVICE", "*DEVICE")
```

```
REPLACE Expr WITH STRTRAN(Expr, "OUTPUT", "*OUTPUT")
REPLACE Expr WITH STRTRAN(Expr, "DEFAULTSOURCE", "*DEFAULTSOURCE")
REPLACE Expr WITH STRTRAN(Expr, "PRINTQUALITY", "*PRINTQUALITY")
REPLACE Expr WITH STRTRAN(Expr, "DUPLEX", "*DUPLEX")
REPLACE Expr WITH STRTRAN(Expr, "YRESOLUTION", "*YRESOLUTION")
REPLACE Expr WITH STRTRAN(Expr, "TTOPTION", "*TTOPTION")
PACK MEMO   && So you don't get memo bloat
```

COM and Office Automation

"COM" stands for Component Object Model, but what it really represents is a great way to build solutions using a variety of tools and allow all the pieces to talk to each other. Many COM servers, such as those that validate data, perform their jobs silently, behind the scenes, but in this chapter we're interested in COM servers for the ways we can use them to present functionality such as that of Microsoft Excel or Microsoft Word from within our Visual FoxPro applications.

To use a COM server such as Excel, instantiate it and make changes to the data using commands similar to the following:

```
*!* Instantiate Excel. We'll make it visible while we're testing.
loExcel = CREATEOBJECT("Excel.Application")
WITH loExcel
  .Visible = .T.

  *!* Now open a file, and write data to it
  .Workbooks.Add("MyWorkbook")
  .Range("A1").Value = "Hello World!"

  *!* Save and exit
  .ActiveWorkbook.SaveAs("MyWorkbook")
  .ActiveWorkbook.Close()
  .Quit()

ENDWITH
RELEASE loExcel
```

When automating Office applications such as Excel, the simplest way to figure out how to proceed is often to go into the application and record a macro of the types of things you wish to do. Then examine the macro in the VBA Editor. You'll get a lot of clues from the macro code about how to program Visual FoxPro to do the same tasks.

Cindy crashed her computer several times when she was first experimenting with Automation, due to having a dozen or so invisible instances of Excel running, each left from a previous crashed program test. Since then she has learned to leave Excel visible during the "crash" phase of testing so it's easy to see whether an instance is still open and clean up the "mess." When everything's working, set the Visible property to .F. for more efficient operation.

Error handling

A good error-handling strategy anticipates problems and handles them gracefully. It's always wise to check that all the parameters have been passed in and that they are of the expected type. Instead of simply opening a table, check whether it is already open with the USED() function.

When checking the results returned from a function or object, test for all return values, even "impossible" ones, and many errors can be avoided or handled transparently to the user.

When an error can't be handled, log the error to a file and perhaps send e-mail to the programmer; then present the user with some choices including retrying the action, ignoring the error and continuing, or exiting the application. If it is unlikely that the user can resolve the problem, inform the user that the application is shutting down, then exit. Be sure to determine whether it may be safe to proceed; you may be able to abort the current function, yet continue with the application itself.

When presenting error messages, it is important to not insult or embarrass the user. Speak to the user in layperson's terms, not technical or database terms a user would not be expected to be familiar with. In other words, use terms from the application domain. Instead of a message like "Fatal error, PatLab not found!" give the user a more pleasant and meaningful message such as "The Patient Lab Results table is unavailable. Please contact the system administrator by phoning the help desk at 555-1234. The application will now close."

See Chapter 9, "Testing and Debugging the Solution," for a further discussion of errors and error handling.

Errors in COM objects

Error handling with COM components is especially important because usually the components have no user interface, and they may be running on computers with no human operator. In a conventional desktop application, you can display options to the user (or at least inform them that the application is closing) if your program can't determine what to do in the case of a particular error, and the user can then decide which action to take. In contrast, COM components must recover from errors without outside intervention because COM .DLLs can't have a user interface. In the case of COM .EXEs that don't specifically handle wait states, any situation awaiting user intervention will put the component into a wait state and make it unavailable to other users. We'll talk more about COM error handling in Chapter 6, "Creating and Managing COM Components," and again in Chapter 9, "Testing and Debugging the Solution."

Providing online Help

Help shouldn't be an afterthought of an application. Plan for the Help files to be the meat of the manual rather than a supplement to it, and make them available to be printed, so the users can add their own notes.

HTML Help has replaced WinHelp and FoxPro's .DBF-style Help as the standard for Windows applications. HTML Help is an improvement over WinHelp because it supports HTML, ActiveX, Java, scripting, .JPGs, .GIFs, .PNGs, linking to the Internet, and the ability to see the HTML code for a Help topic, and an improvement over .DBF-style Help, which, though backward compatible, is limited to a single font and no graphics.

Any HTML editor can be used to create the Web pages, and then HTML Help Workshop can be used to compile them into a .CHM file. HTML Help Workshop can be downloaded from **http://msdn.microsoft.com/library/tools/htmlhelp/wkshp/download_main.htm**. If you find it difficult to use, consider getting West Wind Help Builder from **www.west-wind.com/**. Internet Explorer 4 or higher is needed on the users' workstations in order to run HTML Help.

Access the Help files in any of three ways: via a Help menu, context-sensitive Help, or "What's This?" Help. First, specify which Help file your application is using with `SET HELP TO MyHelp.CHM`. Then set individual topics at appropriate places in your application with `SET TOPIC TO AHelpTopicName`. To open the Help file, use the HELP command, specifying the topic name or HelpContextID with code similar to `HELP WITH ... ENDWITH command`, or `HELP ID 123`.

In the Help menu of an application, you can simply use the command `HELP` to bring up the main Help window. You can also assign F1 or another function to bring up Help by using `ON KEY LABEL F1 HELP`.

For context-sensitive Help, set the HelpContextID property for each control on a form to a unique number to give context-sensitive Help for that control. If no HelpContextID is specified, the one for the form will be used when the user accesses Help. In the Help files, assign the HelpContextID number to the appropriate HTML page.

"What's This?" Help is similar to context-sensitive Help in that it allows you to associate a Help topic with a specific control, toolbar, or form. It is also similar to ToolTips in that the Help topics are displayed above the form. To enable "What's This?" Help, set the Min and Max buttons of the form to .F., set the form's WhatsThisHelp property to .T., and ensure that the form's BorderStyle property is not equal to 0. In addition, to show the "What's This?" Help button in the TitleBar, set the WhatsThisButton property of the form to .T. A benefit of this style of Help is that it is available in modal dialogs when the Help menu is disabled. There is an excellent discussion of Help in *Hacker's Guide to Visual FoxPro 6.0*.

Extending functionality through the Windows API

The Windows Application Programming Interface (API) exposes the functionality of Windows via procedures and functions. Because much of what the API allows us to do is not available directly via Visual FoxPro commands, using the Windows API extends the capabilities of our applications. The Windows API is implemented in a series of .DLLs; some commonly used ones are Kernel32.DLL, GDI32.DLL, and User32.DLL.

Through the API we can do such things as raise a Windows event, reboot Windows, send Windows messages, access graphic functions, and get the user name of the current user. For more than 100 examples, see the Visual FoxPro Downloads on the Universal Thread at **www.universalthread.com/**.

The first step in using an API function is the DECLARE statement. The usage is straightforward, but the catch is that API function names are case-sensitive. This is a departure from VFP, which is not case-sensitive. When pointers or structures are required as parameters, you can usually use a VFP string.

A great example of how to use the API is ShellExecute, which allows you to perform an action on a document type. Here's code that shows how to start the default browser and surf to a Web site:

```
*!* Declare the function
DECLARE INTEGER ShellExecute IN Shell32.DLL ;
    INTEGER hWnd, ;
    STRING lpVerb, ;
    STRING lpFile, ;
    STRING lpParameters, ;
    STRING lpDirectory, ;
```

```
    LONG nShowCmd
*!* Open the default browser with a Web site
ShellExecute(0, "Open", "IExplore.EXE", "http://www.hentzenwerke.com", "", 1)
```

Visual FoxPro on the Web

Because of its lightning-fast string handling capabilities, Visual FoxPro is a great language for Web-enabled applications. The Web is all about text and text protocols such as HTML, XML, HTTP, and SOAP. Visual FoxPro leverages its database technology to enable quick transformation of data into text representations such as HTML and XML. Active Server Pages (ASP) allows us to use VBScript or JScript to interact with databases. DHTML provides a better interface than plain HTML. FoxISAPI gives us a performance boost over CGI and ASP.

Dynamic Hyper Text Markup Language (DHTML) is an enhancement to HTML that provides object-oriented access to a Web page, cascading style sheets, dynamic fonts, and improved UI controls. The downside is that Netscape and Internet Explorer support elements of DHTML differently, making it time-consuming to take advantage of this technology.

Active Server Pages is a server-side scripting technology from Microsoft that uses VBScript, a subset of Visual Basic for Applications, or JScript. ASP is simple to use and is installed automatically with Internet Information Server (IIS). ASP code can be created with any text editor or with a GUI tool such as Visual InterDev. ASP code and HTML tags are mixed in the same text document. Though this mixing of code with HTML makes developing small apps simple, large apps can become unwieldy with bits of code sprinkled all over. Fortunately ASP can call COM components, where you then can unleash the full power of Visual FoxPro.

FoxISAPI uses IIS's Internet Server API (ISAPI). FoxISAPI is a server-side technology that is a high-performance alternative to Active Server Pages. Instead of using a scripting language such as VBScript, you use Visual FoxPro COM objects. This allows fast native access to FoxPro instead of slower data access via Open Database Connectivity (ODBC). In addition, this approach works in pure Visual FoxPro so we can take advantage of its OOP power.

eXtensible Markup Language (XML) is text representation of data using tags, similar to HTML, to give meaning to the data itself, as shown by this example:

```
<data>
  <address>
    <name>Sid Vicious</name>
    <street>123 EMI Avenue</street>
  </address>
 <address>
   <name>Nancy Spungeon</name>
   <street>14 Main Street</street>
 </address>
</data>
```

There is nothing new about the basic idea of XML; programmers have been passing text strings using their own formats for years. The strengths of XML are:

- Text that any client can process.

- Text that is firewall-friendly.

- Text that follows a standard, so other applications will produce or consume text in this format.

Rick Strahl's wwXML class, available at **www.west-wind.com**, makes XML particularly easy to work with. This class provides a mechanism for translating from a cursor to XML and back to a cursor again, allowing us to use native Visual FoxPro data handling commands behind our Web interface.

Sample Questions

In your application, you need to check for instances of the "New Customer" form before proceeding. Which of the following code fragments will accomplish this? (Choose all that apply.)

A.

```
llFormOpen = .F.
FOR EACH loForm IN _SCREEN.ActiveForms
  llFormOpen = llFormOpen OR (UPPER(loForm.Caption) = "NEW CUSTOMER")
ENDFOR
RETURN llFormOpen
```

B.

```
llFormOpen = .F.
FOR lnKounter = 1 TO ALEN(_SCREEN.Forms)
  IF UPPER(_SCREEN.Forms(lnKounter).Caption) = "NEW CUSTOMER"
    llFormOpen = .T.
    RETURN .T.
  ENDIF
ENDFOR
RETURN .F.
```

C.

```
IF UPPER(_SCREEN.Forms(1).Caption) = "NEW CUSTOMER"
  RETURN .T.
ELSE
  RETURN .F.
ENDIF
```

Answer: A and B

In your application, you have a report form where the user can choose beginning and ending dates and the particular report to print. There is code in the LostFocus() method of txtEndDate to check for the reasonableness of the entered dates, but according to one user it doesn't seem to fire. What might be the source of the problem?
  A. You know the code in the LostFocus() is correct, so the user must not be describing the problem accurately.
  B. SET CENTURY is OFF, and the centuries don't compare correctly.

C. The user uses the system toolbar to "Undo" her typing very quickly before the LostFocus() can fire.

D. Your custom Print Preview toolbar is available, and the user is always pressing the Print button directly after she types the date in the text box.

Answer: D

You're moving an application from the desktop to the Web and are rewriting some business rule form method code to be built as a COM object. What, if any, changes must you make to the way errors are handled in the code?

A. COM can't handle errors, so you must code carefully to make sure that no errors occur.

B. Add code to trap the errors and use COMRETURNERROR() to populate the object's exception structure so the client can access these properties and present an appropriate message to the user.

C. There is no difference in the way errors are handled in COM objects, and no need to change any code.

D. Add code that electronically pages the server's console operator, notifying him that an error has occurred, and alert the user to wait for him to walk to the server console to respond to the error.

Answer: B

Further reading

- "Application Specification for Microsoft Windows 2000 for Desktop Applications," Chapter 5, "User Interface Fundamentals,"
  http://msdn.microsoft.com/library/default.asp?URL=/library/specs/w2kcli.htm

- "Building Applications with FoxISAPI,"
  www.west-wind.com/presentations/foxisapi/foxisapi.htm

- "Building Distributed Applications with XML Messaging,"
  www.west-wind.com/presentations/XMLMessaging/xmlmessaging.htm

- *Effective Techniques for Application Development with Visual FoxPro 6.0*, Jim Booth and Steve Sawyer, Chapter 7, "Data Manipulation Classes"

- *Effective Techniques for Application Development with Visual FoxPro 6.0*, Jim Booth and Steve Sawyer, Chapter 12, "User Interface Design"

- **http://fox.wikis.com/wc.dll?Wiki~HtMLHelp**

- **http://fox.wikis.com/wc.dll?Wiki~MultiChildFoxProReports~VFP**

- *Hacker's Guide to Visual FoxPro 6.0*, Tamar E. Granor and Ted Roche, "Declare-DLL"

- *Hacker's Guide to Visual FoxPro 6.0*, Tamar E. Granor and Ted Roche, "Help, Set Help, Set("Help"), Set HelpFilter, Set Topic, Set Topic ID"

- *Hacker's Guide to Visual FoxPro 6.0*, Tamar E. Granor and Ted Roche, "HelpContextID"

- "HTML Help Authoring Guide,"
  http://msdn.microsoft.com/library/tools/htmlhelp/chm/guide.htm

- *Internet Applications with Visual FoxPro 6.0*, Rick Strahl

- *MCSD Visual Basic 6 Desktop Exam Cram*, Michael D. MacDonald, Chapter 6, "Interapplication Communications"

- "Microsoft HTML Help,"
  http://msdn.microsoft.com/library/default.asp?URL=/library/tools/htmlhelp/chm/ hh1start.htm

- *Microsoft Office Automation with Visual FoxPro*, Tamar E. Granor and Della Martin

- *Microsoft Visual FoxPro 6.0 Programmer's Guide*, Chapter 16, "Adding OLE"

- *Microsoft Visual FoxPro 6.0 Programmer's Guide*, Chapter 28, "Accessing the Visual FoxPro API"

- *Microsoft Visual FoxPro 6.0 Programmer's Guide*, Part 3, "Creating the Interface"

- *Microsoft Visual FoxPro 6.0 Programmer's Guide*, Part 7, "Creating Help Files"

- "Microsoft Windows Guidelines for Accessible Software Design,"
  www.microsoft.com/enable/dev/guidelines/software.htm

- *Microsoft Windows User Experience,* Microsoft Corporation

- "Using Toolbars in Visual FoxPro," Dave Lehr, Soft Classics, Ltd.,
  http://msdn.microsoft.com/library/default.asp?URL=/library/backgrnd/html/ msdn_foxtool.htm

- "Using XML Data Services in Distributed Applications,"
  www.west-wind.com/presentations/xmlmessaging/xmldataservices.htm

Third-party software

- Frx2Word, a class that changes a Visual FoxPro report into a Word document, by John Koziol, Visual FoxPro Downloads, **www.universalthread.com**, Public domain, .VCX with source code and documentation

- wwXML, a class that creates XML strings, by Rick Strahl,
  www.west-wind.com/wwxml.asp, Freeware, .VCX with source code
  and documentation

Chapter 6
Creating and Managing
COM Components

Microsoft's Component Object Model (COM) is one of those technologies that simply makes sense. It is a natural fit for object-oriented development and n-tier design. COM allows you to make your VFP objects available to other software and programming environments, thus making a flexible technology for business components in the middle tier. We will show how to build COM components, the different types of COM components available, how to register them, and how to manage them with the Component Gallery. As well, we will touch on error-handling issues with COM and special considerations when using COM and Microsoft Transaction Server.

Evan is a fan of the BBC series "Junkyard Wars." Two teams of four people are asked to build a device to perform a specific task. They have about 10 hours, using only items gathered from a scrap yard. The teams only know the simplest of information about what they have to accomplish. The host of the show may ask them to "build a flying machine" or "build a device to raise a car submerged in water." Evan's favorite episode had the two teams building a device to knock down a wall. One team built an A-frame with a pole suspended by chains. One end of the pole had a heavy weight on it, and the team members pulled the pole back and forth using muscle power. The second team built a hydraulic arm with a jaw at the end. To make a long story short, the team with the hydraulic arm lost because their complicated system broke down and because one of the walls had a roof and they were unable to grip it with the jaw. The team with the pole was very slow, but because of the simplicity of the machine, it didn't break down. The pole was versatile as well; they could shorten or lengthen the chains to hit the wall at any point.

With few exceptions, teams win these contests because of the simplicity and versatility of their designs. Simplicity frees the designers to focus on solving the problem rather than on the details of implementing the solution. Versatility allows unexpected situations to be accommodated with fewer system changes. The Component Object Model (COM) and Distributed COM (DCOM) provide Visual FoxPro developers with both simplicity and versatility in deploying applications. Let's look at what they offer us toward making our applications simple and versatile.

What is COM?

COM is a technology that allows a developer to make objects written in a variety of programming languages available to other programming languages and software. COM allows us to deploy an application on a single client computer or across several servers via DCOM.

Simplicity comes from the way COM is implemented. Take a Visual FoxPro class definition and simply add the OLEPUBLIC keyword, and compile the classes into an .EXE or .DLL. Then, you can instantiate the class in any of the following ways:

```
Pure VFP:    oJoe = CREATEOBJECT("Staff")
COM:         oJoe = CREATEOBJECT("ComName.Staff")
DCOM:        oJoe = CREATEOBJECT("DcomName.Staff","MyServer.com")
```

Once an object has been instantiated, it is used in the same way regardless of whether VFP, COM, or DCOM has been used. What could be simpler?

COM offers a variety of choices in how it is deployed. We can host applications locally on a single machine. If necessary, we can switch to DCOM when an application needs to be shared by more than one user via a server.

Because COM is used for implementing objects, it is a natural fit for object-oriented programming (OOP) used in Visual FoxPro.

Creating COM components

Because COM components can be deployed locally and then scaled up to remote servers, they are ideal for encapsulating business rules in the business tier. As long as all software uses the COM business components to access data, rather than accessing the data directly, you can be sure that your business rules are being respected. The business rules are easy to spot in **Listing 1**, and because they are centralized in the component, they are easy to change should the business rules change.

Listing 1. COM component showing business rules for adding patients.

```
DEFINE CLASS Patient AS SESSION OLEPUBLIC
  * Adds new patient to database
  * Returns .T. if successful
  * Returns .F. if a business rule is violated

  DATASESSION = 2     && private datasession

  PROCEDURE Init
    USE Patients SHARED in 0
  ENDPROC

  PROCEDURE Destroy
    USE IN Patients
  ENDPROC

  PROCEDURE AddData
    LARAMETERS pcName, pnAge

    * Patient name must not be blank
    IF ALLTRIM(pcName) == ""
      RETURN .F.
    ENDIF

    * Patient must be 18 or over
    IF pnAge < 18
      RETURN .F.
    ENDIF

    * No business rule violated, add data to database
    SELECT Patients
```

```
     INSERT INTO Patients (FullName, Age) VALUES (pcName, pnAge)
     RETURN .T.
   ENDPROC

ENDDEFINE
```

COM server types

COM components can be created as in-process or out-of-process. In-process components can be single-threaded or multi-threaded. At compile time, you choose which type of component to build: out-of-process .EXE, single-threaded in-process .DLL, or multi-threaded in-process .DLL.

An in-process component is a .DLL that runs in the same address space as the program that calls it. In-process components run faster because there is no inter-process communication. The downside is that a crash in the .DLL can crash the calling client. In addition, to update a .DLL that is part of a Web application, you must shut down the Web server. The only way to run an in-process component on a remote computer is via MTS. A multi-threaded .DLL can increase responsiveness of the application, especially if there are long processes on the system, because the shorter processes will be able to interrupt the long process and give the users the impression that the system has a better response time. Multi-threading comes at the cost of overhead of managing the processes.

An out-of-process component is an .EXE that runs in a separate process from the calling client. Though slower than a .DLL (as mentioned previously), a crash on the server won't bring down the client. An .EXE can be updated without stopping the Web server. The out-of-process component can run on a remote computer via DCOM.

Business rules

Business rules are the constraints of the system that you are modeling. Examples of business rules are:

- Every invoice must have at least one product on it.

- All patients must be 18 years or older.

- Customers paying by check must provide three pieces of identification.

The component is then compiled into a COM .DLL called BIZCOM.DLL. **Listing 2** shows an example of its use in VFP. Put all of the components and tables into one directory and SET DEFAULT TO that directory. Evan uses session-based classes rather than custom-based because it allows him to set private data sessions. This means that for non-COM-based applications, the data manipulations in the objects won't affect each other. Also, it means that he can use these class definitions in a pure VFP environment or a COM environment.

Listing 2. *Using a COM component with good and bad data.*

```
* Instantiate the CLASS as an object
oPatient = CREATEOBJECT("BizCom.Patient")

* Add a patient
IF oPatient.AddData("Humphrey Bogart", 82) = .T.
  MESSAGEBOX("Data saved")
ELSE
   MESSAGEBOX("Data not saved")
ENDIF
* Attempt to add another patient that breaks the rules
IF oPatient.AddData("Orphan Annie", 5) = .T.
  MESSAGEBOX("Data saved")
ELSE
  MESSAGEBOX("Data not saved")
ENDIF

* Release the object
RELEASE oPatient
```

Interacting with other components

COM components can call each other to delegate responsibility from one to another. **Listing 3** shows the oEmployee object delegating the lookup of the department name to the oDept object. **Listing 4** shows how the method is called in code. We purposefully haven't listed the code for the oDept object because we don't care how it is implemented. All we know is that we pass it an employee primary ID and it sends back the department name. The object could be getting the data out of a VFP table on the C:\ drive, or from a SQL Server table half a world away!

Listing 3. *The oEmployee object delegates department name lookup to the oDept object.*

```
DEFINE CLASS Employee AS SESSION OLEPUBLIC
  * Employee Biz object
  DATASESSION = 2  && private datasession

  PROCEDURE Init
    USE Employee SHARED IN 0
  ENDPROC

  PROCEDURE Destroy
    USE IN Employee
  ENDPROC

  PROCEDURE GetDeptName
    LPARAMETERS pnEmployeePK
    LOCAL lcDeptName

    * Get the department foreign key from employee table
    * Returns department name if found
    IF NOT USED("Employee")
      USE Employee IN 0
    ENDIF
```

```
   IF SEEK(pnEmployeePK, "Employee", "pkId")
      * Delegate retrieving the department name to oDept object
      oDept = CREATEOBJECT("Dept")
      lcDeptName = oDept.GetName(Employee.fkDept)
      RELEASE oDept
      RETURN lcDeptName
   ELSE
      RETURN "Employee not found"
   ENDIF
  ENDPROC
ENDDEFINE
```

Listing 4. *Using the GetDeptName() method of the oEmployee object.*

```
* Instantiate the employee business class
oEmployee = CREATEOBJECT("BizCom.Employee")

* Get the dept names for employees with primary keys 1, 2, 4, 5
? oEmployee.GetDeptName(1)
? oEmployee.GetDeptName(2)
? oEmployee.GetDeptName(4)
? oEmployee.GetDeptName(5)

* Release the employee object from memory
RELEASE oEmployee
```

COM error handling

Error handling with COM components is especially important because often the components have no user interface and they can be running on computers with no human operator. In a conventional application, if your program can't determine what to do in the case of a particular error, you can display the options to the user. This may be something like the classic "The staff data cannot be accessed, would you like to Retry, Ignore, or Cancel?" The user can try one or more of the options to see whether anything works before calling tech support or rebooting. A COM component can only report the error back to the calling component and log the error. If a message were to display on a COM .EXE component running on a server, it could lock the component because an error message would pop on the server's monitor. Without anyone there to press a Continue or OK button, the component would be stuck and couldn't respond to requests. You can prevent a component from having a wait state (such as an error message from an unhandled error) by using SYS(2335). COM .DLL components cannot and do not natively have any UI capabilities, so SYS(2335) is unnecessary.

A good error-handling strategy anticipates problems and handles them gracefully. It's always a good idea to check that all the parameters have been passed in and that they are of the expected type. Instead of simply opening a table, check whether it is already open with the USED() function. When checking the results returned from a function or object, test for all return values, even "impossible" ones. Though we are discussing COM error handling, this advice applies to error handling for all types of applications.

For errors that can't be anticipated, a good strategy will return as much information as possible and bow out gracefully. Every class definition should have code in its Error() method, which fires automatically when an error occurs. This differs from a conventional application, where you have to invoke an error handler with the ON ERROR command. When the object's Error event fires, the Error() method should try to handle all the errors that are specific to the class. Any that it can't handle can be passed up the class hierarchy. If the parent class can't handle the error, an error-handling class can be called.

The function COMRETURNERROR() lets our COM components raise errors. The beauty of this mechanism is that the client tier doesn't have to have to handle COM errors differently than errors that occur inside of the client tier itself. The error information is gathered using AERROR(). **Listing 5** shows how to use COMRETURNERROR() and also demonstrates one method of logging the error to a file. In Listing 5, we're trying to keep the example simple; in a real component, you want to try to handle the error locally if you can.

Listing 5. *Component showing COM error handling and logging.*

```
DEFINE CLASS Invoice AS SESSION OLEPUBLIC
  * Invoice Biz object
  * Demonstrates COM error handling
    PROCEDURE DoSomething(pnDeptPK)
    * generate a fake error using the error command
    ERROR "A really terrible error"
  ENDPROC

  PROCEDURE Error(pnErrorNum, pcMethodName, pnLineNum)
    LOCAL lcErrorMess

  * To keep example simple, don't handle error, pass it back to
  * calling application
    lcErrorMess = ;
      DTOC(DATETIME())+ ;
      " | Error Number:" + TRANSFORM(pnErrorNum) + ;
      " | Method Name:" + pcMethodName + ;
      " | Line Number:" + TRANSFORM(pnLineNum) + ;
      " | Message:" + message()
    * Append to error log text file
    STRTOFILE(lcErrorMess + chr(13), "error.log", .t. )
    * Raise a COM error to notify client
    * The client will handle the error as instructed
    COMRETURNERROR("MyServer",lcErrorMess)
  ENDPROC
ENDDEFINE
```

Listing 6 shows that, in the client code, COM errors are handled exactly the same as other VFP errors. In this code fragment, we simply display the error information, though in a real application we would probably choose to handle the error more gracefully.

Listing 6. *COM error handling at the client.*

```
ON ERROR ErrorHandler()   && Enable error handler

* Instantiate invoice class to an object
oInvoice = CREATEOBJECT("BizCom.Invoice")
```

```
nResult = oInvoice.DoSomething(1)

PROCEDURE ErrorHandler()
  DIMENSION laError[1]

  * Load error info into an array
  * In a real application we would try to handle the error
  AERROR(laError)
  LcErrorMessage = ""
  FOR i = 1 TO 7
    LcErrorMessage = lcErrorMessage + laError(i) + CHR(13)
  ENDFOR

  MESSAGEBOX(lcErrorMessage)
ENDPROC
```

Designing components for MTS

Microsoft Transaction Server (MTS) is a run-time environment for COM components that allows caching of the components to improve performance. For background on what MTS is and why you would want to use it, see Randy Brown's article "Microsoft Transaction Server for Visual FoxPro Developers" in the MSDN Library, as listed in the "Further reading" section at the end of this chapter.

When designing COM components to be used with MTS, we need to consider the following:

- Stateless components that don't rely on state being saved are more efficient in MTS.

- COM components used in MTS must be in-process .DLLs.

- SetComplete and SetAbort methods let MTS know when you won't need the component for a while.

Stateless components are more efficient for MTS because the context of the component doesn't need to be restored each time the component is called. This means less work for the server, meaning that the server can handle more requests and scale better. As our tech editor spotted, the code samples earlier in the chapter are statefull because they rely on the data tables being opened in the Init() method of the object. For a discussion of state and statelessness, see **http://msdn.microsoft.com/library/techart/d3dalchg.htm**.

Only in-process COM .DLLs run in MTS. Simple, out-of-process .EXEs simply don't run in MTS, so recompile your components into .DLLs.

Even if we aren't using transactions, SetComplete and SetAbort tell MTS that the object we are using can become stateless. This allows MTS to deactivate the object and free up resources on the server. At the end of each object method, issue SetComplete before the RETURN statement.

Transaction support for COM components in MTS

MTS supports database transactions via Distributed Transaction Coordinator (DTC). Both Microsoft SQL Server and Oracle are supported, but unfortunately Visual FoxPro database transactions are not. With Visual FoxPro tables, the objects must manage the transactions. DTC means that transactions are handled by MTS and that transactions can be committed or rolled back over heterogeneous systems databases and servers. Before DTC, the developer had to manage these potentially complex transactions himself.

To begin a transaction, call GetObjectContext(.T.). Then, do the database operations. Finally, call SetComplete() to commit the transaction or SetAbort() to revert it.

Managing and deploying COM components

Now that we have talked about developing COM components, let's look behind the scenes at building and managing the components. We'll look at using the Component Gallery to manage components, COM server types, registering components, and creating and management packages with MTS Explorer.

Using the Component Gallery

The Component Gallery is accessed from the Tools | Component Gallery menu option. The Gallery is an interface for grouping components into categories called "catalogs." Catalogs are pointers or shortcuts to the actual components, and they can be further broken down into folders. They offer us a convenient way to organize not only components, but other classes, projects, and really just about anything. Each catalog is a .DBF file. The Component Gallery is just another tool for helping to organize VFP development. It is pan-project and goes beyond just .VCX-based classes like the Class Browser.

To add a new catalog:

1. Click the Options button on the toolbar.

2. Click the Catalogs tab (see **Figure 1**).

3. Click the New... button (see **Figure 2**).

4. Type a catalog name and location.

5. Click the Save button.

6. Click OK to leave the Options dialog.

To add a new folder:

1. Choose (in the left pane) the catalog to which you want to add a folder.

2. Right-click on the right pane of the Component Gallery.

3. Choose New Item, then Folder.

4. Right-click on the folder called "New Folder," and then click Properties.

5. Enter a name and description, and then click the OK button.

To add a component to a catalog:

1. Choose the catalog or folder to add to.

2. Right-click on the right pane.

3.   Select New Item, then the type of component (Activex, Class, Datasource, File, Form, Image, Menu, Program, Project, Report, Sample, Web Site).

4.   Browse to find the component, and then click the OK button.

5.   Right-click the component, and choose Properties to add a description and icon.

You can set various options in the Component Gallery by clicking the Options button on the toolbar. A handy feature is that you can drag components into your VFP projects.

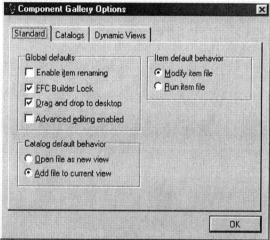

Figure 1. *The Component Gallery Options Standard tab. You can choose the default behavior when a component is clicked.*

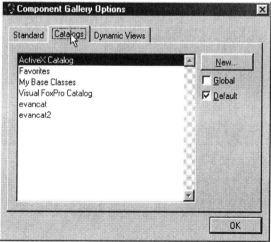

Figure 2. *The Component Gallery Options Catalogs tab. Evan has added his own catalogs.*

Registering and unregistering COM components

COM components must be registered with Windows (that is, in the Registry) before you can use them. For .EXE components:

- Register by using `MyExe /regserver`

- Unregister with `MyExe /unregserver`

For .DLL components:

- Register with `REGSVR32 MyDll.DLL`

- Unregister with `REGSVR32 /u MyDll.DLL`

Creating packages and managing components with MTS Explorer

MTS lets you browse the components registered on a machine. See Chapter 10, "Deploying an Application," for more details. Also, see the Microsoft white paper, "Microsoft Management Console: Overview," which is referenced in the "Further reading" section of this chapter.

Following are some common things that are done with MTS Explorer (also called Microsoft Management Console). **Figure 3** shows the layout of Microsoft Management Console, a familiar interface to those who are accustomed to using to Windows Explorer.

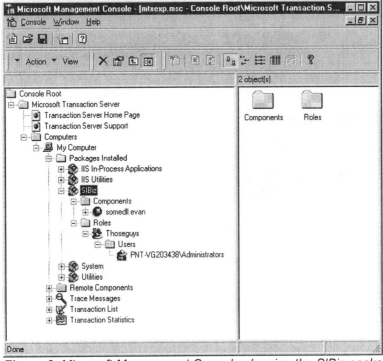

Figure 3. *Microsoft Management Console showing the SIBiz package.*

To create an empty package:

1. From the command line, run MMC (Microsoft Management Console).

2. Navigate down the tree in the left pane to "Packages Installed" (see Figure 3).

3. On the toolbar, choose Create A New Object.

4. Choose Create An Empty Package.

5. Type in a name for the package, and then choose Next.

6. Select the users that can use this package, and then choose Finish.

To add a component to a package:

1. In the left pane, select the package.

2. Select the component folder under the package.

3. Use Windows Explorer to find your component.

4. Drag and drop it into the right pane.

Using role-based security

MTS allows you to leverage Windows NT and Windows 2000's security features using role-based security. A role is a group of users that can access an MTS component.

To add a role to a package:

1. Under the package in the left pane, select the subfolder Roles.

2. Right-click the subfolder and select New, then Roles.

3. Type in a name for the role, then click OK.

4. In the left pane, select your role, and then select the subfolder Users.

5. Right-click and select New, then User.

6. Select each user, and then click Add. Do this for each user you need to add to the group.

7. Click OK.

Sample Question

You need to register a component called TheDLL.DLL. Which syntax will do the job?
A. TheDLL.DLL /R
B. TheDLL.DLL /Reg
C. REGSVR32 /R TheDLL.DLL
D. REGSVR32 TheDLL.DLL

Answer: D

Further reading

- *Internet Applications with Visual FoxPro 6.0*, Rick Strahl, Chapter 9, "Visual FoxPro and COM"

- "Error Handling in Visual FoxPro," Doug Hennig, includes article and extensive code for handling errors during execution, **www.stonefield.com/pub/errorh.zip**

- **http://fox.wikis.com/wc.dll?Wiki~ComErrorHandling**

- **http://fox.wikis.com/wc.dll?Wiki~COMComponentExample**

- **http://fox.wikis.com/wc.dll?Wiki~ComReturnError**

- **http://fox.wikis.com/wc.dll?Wiki~ComErrors**

- **http://fox.wikis.com/wc.dll?Wiki~ErrorEventStrategy**

- "Microsoft Management Console: Overview," white paper, **http://microsoft.com/windows2000/library/howitworks/management/mmcover.asp**

- "Microsoft Transaction Server for Visual FoxPro Developers," Randy Brown, Microsoft Corporation, **http://msdn.microsoft.com/library/default.asp?URL=/library/techart/mtsvfp.htm**

- "Using Microsoft Transaction Server With VFP," Rick Strahl, **www.west-wind.com/presentations/mts/mts.htm**

- **http://fox.wikis.com/wc.dll?Wiki~SettingUpMTS**

- "How Microsoft Transaction Server Changes the COM Programming Model," David Chappell, **http://msdn.microsoft.com/library/periodic/period98/mtsjan.htm**

- **http://fox.wikis.com/wc.dll?Wiki~UsingAndDevelopingForMTS**

- "The Microsoft Component Gallery," Steven M. Black, **http://msdn.microsoft.com/library/default.asp?URL=/library/techart/Vfpgallery.htm**

- *Advanced Object Oriented Programming with Visual FoxPro 6.0*, Markus Egger, Chapter 5, "OOP Standards"

- *The Fundamentals: Building Visual Studio Applications on a Visual FoxPro 6.0 Foundation*, Whil Hentzen, Chapter 17, "The Component Gallery"

- *Hacker's Guide to Visual FoxPro 6.0*, Tamar Granor and Ted Roche, "Hacking the Class Browser and the Component Gallery"

Chapter 7
Creating Data Services

In Chapter 2, "The Logical Data Model," we concerned ourselves with the logical data model for our application: that is, what data we would need to store, and how the various data entities would interact. Here we discuss the ways we plan to move data into and out of our back-end data store, either one record at a time or in a transaction that might affect multiple fields in multiple tables. Only after all of this is done do we actually design the database, as described in Chapter 8, "Creating a Physical Database."

When working with data, we need to concern ourselves with issues such as how competing changes to the same record might be handled, how updates that should cascade throughout our data might be accomplished, and how we might present compiled data, such as a monthly average or total, to the user. We will also concern ourselves with appropriate ways to interact with non-native data.

The simplest way to interact with data is to use native FoxPro tables and edit them directly, but this approach isn't the best way to build a robust, scalable system. Our goal is to design for a layer between the user and the data that allows changes to be undone, and to design so that multiple changes can be made together or undone together if part of the update fails. We also want to design so that we can easily change from one type of back-end database to another should our needs change. We'll want to accomplish these using the built-in capabilities that Visual FoxPro offers us, such as buffering, rules, triggers, and stored procedures, so that the integrity of our data is protected when it is accessed apart from the application we're designing. We also want to be sure that we are able to access any type of foreign data.

Native tables, views, SQL pass-through, ADO, and OLE DB

Toward our goal of a robust, scalable application, we want to make our data access methods as flexible as possible. Views allow us to treat FoxPro free tables, FoxPro database tables, and foreign data in much the same way. We can interact with our views by using familiar, fast, Xbase commands.

We can also interact with ODBC-compliant data entirely via SQL pass-through technology (SPT, a technology where the SQL commands, in string form, are passed directly to the database server without further interpretation by the client), which also allows us to perform operations on foreign data stores such as creating or modifying tables, or calling stored procedures.

Finally, we can access data through Microsoft's newest data access technology, ActiveX Data Objects, or ADO. Form controls, with the exception of the grid, can be bound to ADO recordsets. The Microsoft FlexGrid ActiveX control can be used where grid functionality is desired. The ADO technology, together with the new OLE DB data providers, allows access to many varied data stores in a consistent way, without the upkeep of installing ODBC data sources on each client machine. Beyond this, the Remote Data Services (RDS) technology allows access to data anywhere on the Internet!

We'll be spending the majority of our time on the more commonly used data access technologies—remote views and SQL pass-through—and then covering ADO, OLE DB, and RDS.

Connecting to the data

When we're using native tables or local views, we're already connected to our data, but both remote views and SQL pass-through require a connection to the back-end data store before we can use the data. Remote views require that the connection be defined and named in the .DBC or that a named data source be used, while the SQL pass-through process begins with the SQLCONNECT() function, which can also use a named connection or a connection string, or the SQLSTRINGCONNECT() function, which uses a connection string. The advantage of named connections is that maintenance is easily done in one place for all views or SPT using that data source.

Data access

In Visual FoxPro, we can move beyond the SCATTER and GATHER we used to use as a safety layer between the user and the data, to views, which allow us to edit multiple records from multiple tables and package all of the changes into one update. In addition, views offer us a way to take advantage of some of the capabilities of the Visual FoxPro database container when we access FoxPro 2.6 tables. We also have native access to SQL pass-through commands that we can use to add, delete, or modify data. Finally, we can set the properties of a cursor resulting from SQL pass-through so that it's updatable, and use it in much the same way that we use a view.

Visual FoxPro allows us to access foreign data via the SQL programming language through ODBC drivers that are provided by the makers of those foreign databases. Examples are data housed in a Microsoft SQL Server database or an Oracle database. Each of these databases, as well as Visual FoxPro, supports a subset or superset of the ANSI/ISO Standard SQL-92 language, so it is important, and very worthwhile, for the developer to be well versed in SQL in general and to understand what is and is not supported by the particular SQL installations he works with. We'll be going into more detail on SQL commands in the "SQL syntax for creating views or selecting data" section later in this chapter.

By using views to access native data, we pave the way for an easy transition to an SQL database, and by sticking to the standard SQL language, we eliminate problems that might arise when a customer decides to move from a Visual FoxPro .DBC to an SQL database, or to change from one SQL database to another to house his data. Microsoft calls moving data from Visual FoxPro tables to an SQL database "upsizing" and provides the Upsizing Wizard to help with this chore.

Finally, views look just like native tables to Visual FoxPro. We can use any of the familiar, fast, Xbase commands with our local and remote views and SPT cursors.

Xbase commands for data

Xbase commands for navigating through data include LOCATE, SEEK, SEEK() and INDEXSEEK(), SKIP, and SCAN...ENDSCAN. Commands for changing data include APPEND BLANK, REPLACE, GATHER, and DELETE. How you choose to use them will depend a lot on your data and your programming goals: usually a mixture of clarity and maintainability, speed, and scalability.

For ease of programming and clarity for those who may maintain your code, SCAN...ENDSCAN (possibly including a FOR clause on the SCAN) is a nice way to work through records in a table or parameterized view. For really large native tables, consider setting an order in the table, using SEEK, and following it with SCAN WHILE...ENDSCAN to speed things up by stepping through the fewest possible records. You'll have to find the point where added speed justifies the extra code in your own particular situation.

If you feel that your application may someday move to an SQL back end, you may want to consider using INSERT-SQL, UPDATE-SQL, and DELETE-SQL instead of the sometimes-faster Xbase APPEND BLANK, REPLACE, GATHER, and DELETE on any code that may someday become a server stored procedure. Otherwise, when you're working on local data, whether it's VFP data, views, or cursors created from remote data, there's no reason to prefer SQL commands for manipulation within the program. In fact, that's one of the big benefits of using VFP. You can use Xbase commands on data from other sources. We'll talk more about the SQL commands later in the "SQL syntax for modifying data" section.

Finally, since SEEK and SEEK() move the record pointer, potentially causing an unwanted TABLEUPDATE() to occur or a trigger to fire, INDEXSEEK() has been added to our toolbox in VFP6. It's the fastest way to determine the presence of a particular record in a table or cursor, and it doesn't move the record pointer unless told to do so. Best of all, these commands don't depend on knowing or being in the current work area, or knowing the current order or having an order set at all.

Views

Think of a view as a peephole through which you can see data. The back-end data determines whether a view is local or remote. If the back end is Visual FoxPro or FoxPro tables, another view, or a combination of either of those with remote data, it is a local view. A view of data accessed by an ODBC connection is a remote view. A special type of view, called an offline view, is used in situations like those that occur when a salesman takes a laptop on the road. Using the CREATEOFFLINE() function, the data is selected, stored locally and available for editing, and then synched up with the main database later with the ONLINE keyword of the USE command. Conflicts with back-end data that has changed while the local data was offline must be anticipated and handled in code.

In general, a view can be accessed, and behaves, much like a native table. The view itself is based on a temporary table that disappears when it is closed or when the application finishes. Any added indexes are lost when the view is closed and must be re-created each time. Views can be created and maintained through the GUI interface of the View Designer, or entirely in code.

A view can allow access to all records in the tables involved, be parameterized to retrieve and show only data that meets certain criteria selected at run time, permanently filtered to show only certain types of records, or constructed to show compiled data such as counts, averages, or totals. Views are an excellent way to show data from more than one table. Though this is not a good strategy to use when updating data, it's an excellent strategy for browsing or reporting. A view can even be constructed to combine both local and remote data. The behavior of a view is determined by its properties, set temporarily with CURSORSETPROP() or permanently with DBSETPROP().

Local views

The syntax for creating and using a local view is:

```
CREATE SQL VIEW MyView AS <SQL SELECT statement>
Use MyView IN 0
```

We'll discuss the details of the SELECT… syntax, including how to ask for a parameter, later in the "SQL for creating views or selecting data" section, and the details of locking, buffering, and transactions in the "Locking, buffering, and transactions to prevent update conflicts" section. For now, though, that's what you need to know to create and use a local view.

Remote views

Before you can set up a remote view, you must either set up a connection in your database or set up a data source on the client machine. If you're using the Visual FoxPro View Designer, it prompts you for one of these as you begin. The details of creating the connection are covered in Chapter 8, "Creating a Physical Database," and the details of the SQL SELECT statement are in the "SELECT – SQL" section later in this chapter. Setting up a data source is beyond the scope of this book, but the Windows ODBC Data Source Administrator is pretty easy to use.

Here's the syntax for a remote view:

```
CREATE SQL VIEW MyView REMOTE CONNECTION MyConnection AS <SQL SELECT statement>
```

If you're not using a connection in the database, you can refer to the data source directly:

```
CREATE SQL VIEW MyView REMOTE CONNECTION MyDataSource AS <SQL SELECT statement>
```

SQL pass-through

SQL pass-through is a technique that sends a command to the back-end database in string format, and the action is performed at the server, with any results returned to the client.

You must connect to the server and get a "handle" for the connection, and close it when you're done. If there's an error, you can trap for it. You might use commands like the following:

```
*!* Make the connection and get the handle
nConnectionHandle = SQLCONNECT("MyConnection")

IF nConnectionHandle <= 0
    = MESSAGEBOX("Cannot make connection", 16, "SQL Connect Error")
```

```
*!* Successful connection, proceed with execution
*!* Assumes cSQLCommandString is a valid SQL command
ELSE
  nDidIExecute = SQLEXEC(nConnectionHandle, cSQLCommandString, "SQLResults")

  *!* During testing, trap for execution errors, usually caused by the
  *!* SQL syntax. Otherwise, we were successful in retrieving data.
  IF nDidIExecute < 0
    = AERROR(MyErrorArray)
    MESSAGEBOX(STR(MyErrorArray(1)) + CHR(13) + ;
      MyErrorArray(2), 64, "SQLEXEC Error Message")
  ENDIF

  *!* Close the connection. Zero parameter closes ALL connections.
  = SQLDISCONNECT(0)
ENDIF
```

When building the command string to pass in SQLEXEC(), add clarity and avoid errors by using square brackets as character string delimiters and build the string in pieces. Watch out for spacing problems:

```
cSelect = [SELECT * FROM MyTable ]
cWhere = [WHERE SomeField = "Some character value" ] + ;
  [AND SomeOtherCondition = .T. ]
cOrderBy = [ORDER BY Field1, Field2, Field3 ]

cSQLCommandString = cSelect + cWhere + cOrderBy

lWasISuccessful = SQLEXEC(lnHandle, cSQLCommandString, "ResultCursor")
```

Use the UPDATE command to send updates to the server:

```
cUpdate = [UPDATE MyTable ]
cSet = [SET SomeField = "Some character value", ] + ;
  [SomeOtherField = ] + STR(nSomeNumericValue) + [ ]
cWhere = [MyTable.KeyField = ] + STR(nMyKey) + [ ]

cSQLCommandString = cUpdate + cSet + cWhere

lWasISuccessful = SQLEXEC(lnHandle, cSQLCommandString)
```

An alternative to the UPDATE command (in Help as UPDATE – SQL) is to modify the non-updatable cursor to be an updatable cursor with code similar to the following:

```
SQLEXEC(lnHandle, cSQLCommandString, "MyCursor")   && Retrieve the data

*!* SELECT MyCursor   && Should be selected unless you've done other work first

*!* Define scope for UpdateNameList
CURSORSETPROP("Tables", "MyTable")
*!* Pair cursor field names for the key field and any fields you want to update
*!* with back-end Table.Field names
CURSORSETPROP("UpdateNameList", "TableNo MyTable.TableNo")
*!* Local names of key fields to be used for updates, ours is "TableNo"
CURSORSETPROP("KeyFieldList", "TableNo")
```

```
*!* Names of fields in back-end that will be updated, ours is "TableNo"
CURSORSETPROP("UpdatableFieldList", "TableNo")
*!* Make cursor updatable
CURSORSETPROP("SendUpdates", .T.)

*!* Make changes to cursor records here

TABLEUPDATE(.T., .T.)
```

SQL syntax for creating views or selecting data

SQL is a very powerful language, and it's worth learning. As we mentioned earlier in the "Data access" section, Visual FoxPro uses a subset/superset of ANSI SQL-92, and by sticking to standard SQL commands you can avoid problems when upsizing views to an SQL database, or when the back-end database changes. There are books on the market that deal with standard SQL and specific installations of it, as well as examples of commands for special situations. Cindy's favorite is *Joe Celko's SQL For Smarties, Second Edition*.

SELECT – SQL

The SQL SELECT command (in Help as SELECT – SQL) is used for creating views, in SQL pass-through to retrieve data, and for internal data selection for such purposes as reporting. Since the View Designer has limitations and can't be used at all for SQL pass-through, an understanding of the processes of joining tables, aggregating fields, and grouping records entirely in code is essential to selecting the data we want, exactly as we want it. The Help for SELECT – SQL is detailed, but it's often difficult to picture what data we want, and how to apply our understanding of SQL to write the command to retrieve it.

We begin with the keyword SELECT and follow it with a list of the fields we want. The list can include user-defined functions, aggregates such as COUNT() or SUM(), and FoxPro functions like NVL() or IIF(), with aliases for the resulting fields. (When using ANSI SQL-92, substitute COALESCE() for NVL() and CASE for IIF().)

WHERE and JOIN

We can retrieve data from multiple tables through the WHERE and JOIN clauses, with the WHERE clause offering the same functionality as an INNER JOIN. The functionality of OUTER joins can be simulated by careful use of WHERE and UNION clauses, but we'll spend our time here on the JOIN syntax and the results it gives.

LEFT OUTER JOIN gives all of the records from the "parent" table on the left, and matching records from the "child" table on the right. If there are no child matches for the parent, NULLs are put into the child fields. NVL() can be used to retrieve blanks or zeros instead of NULLs when there are no matching child records. Orphan child records are not selected. RIGHT OUTER JOIN is the inverse if it's easier to conceptualize the joins in that manner.

A FULL JOIN gives all of the records from both joined tables. Where records are unmatched, there are NULLs in fields that are not shared between the two tables. The FULL JOIN returns a record for each match between the two tables, plus each unmatched record from the left-side table (nulls for fields from the right side), plus each unmatched record from the right-side table (nulls for fields from the left side).

In addition to allowing us to join tables (equivalent to INNER JOIN), the WHERE clause lets us filter our data. If we're writing SQL to retrieve data, we can easily pick up our parameters from a value input by the user, as in the following:

```
lnStartYear = THISFORM.txtStartYear.VALUE
lnEndYear   = THISFORM.txtEndYear.VALUE

cSQLCommandString = ;
  [SELECT * FROM MyTable WHERE nMyYear BETWEEN ] + ;
  lnStartYear + [ AND ] + lnEndYear + [ ]

*!* Use this syntax for SQL pass-through
*!* SQLEXEC(lnHandle, cSQLCommandString, "SQLResults")

*!* Use this syntax for internal selection such as for a report
*!* &cSQLCommandString
```

If we're writing SQL for a view, however, either through the GUI View Designer or in code, we can let Visual FoxPro prompt the user for the parameter value by preceding it with a question mark as shown in **Figure 1**.

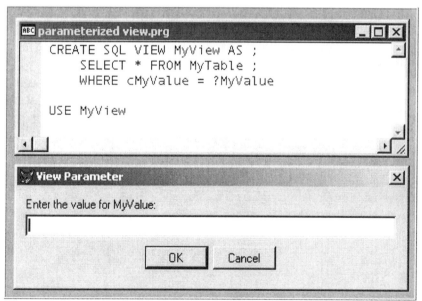

Figure 1. Visual FoxPro automatically prompts us for a view parameter if the parameter is preceded by a question mark.

In reality though, the developer usually uses a form text box to capture the parameter value, and passes it to the view as a variable as shown in **Figure 2**. This avoids the look of the automatic prompt.

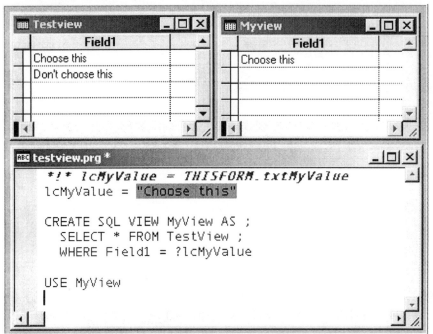

Figure 2. *Capturing the value of a view parameter in a form text box and passing it to the parameterized view avoids the automatic prompt. Though you wouldn't normally create a view on the fly like this, we wanted you to see how a view parameter could be passed in using the question mark notation in the view definition, and having the parameter in scope when the view is opened.*

Aggregates

Aggregates are functions such as SUM() or COUNT() that compile values from several records into one. Note carefully the interaction of null values with aggregate functions as illustrated in **Figure 3**. Aggregates ignore null values, with the exception of COUNT(*), which actually uses system information rather than table values. If GROUP BY is not included, the aggregate includes all selected records, and one record is returned.

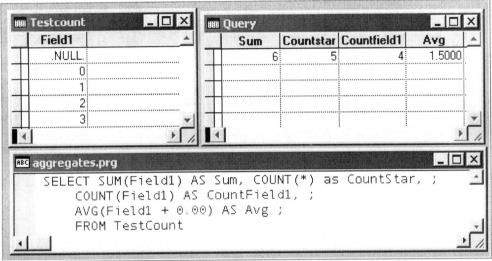

Figure 3. Note carefully the interaction of null values and aggregate functions. COUNT(*) counts records so records with null values are included. They are totally ignored in the SUM() and AVERAGE() functions.

ORDER BY

ORDER BY lets you determine the order of the data in the view. It's especially useful when an index would require converting date or numeric data types to strings. This ORDER BY clause organizes the view by customer name, then by order number within each customer, and finally by payment date within each order:

```
ORDER BY cCustName, nOrderNumber, dPaymentDate
```

Often the view or cursor is small enough that LOCATE can be used and indexes done away with entirely. This approach is especially attractive because indexes on views have to be created each time the view is opened.

Use the DESCENDING keyword to indicate that ordering on a particular field should be reversed, for example, to have the most recent payments shown earlier in the list. ORDER BY is also a requirement when selecting something like the top sales figures. Again, use the DESCENDING keyword with TOP to get the lowest values.

GROUP BY and HAVING

Two more SQL clauses, GROUP BY and HAVING, go a long way toward determining the results of our selection.

The GROUP BY clause of the SELECT statement allows us to aggregate our data, or allows us to retrieve fewer records. The most often overlooked issue with the GROUP BY clause is that in ANSI SQL-92, all of the selected fields, except those that are aggregated, must be listed in the GROUP BY clause. VFP's SQL does not require this, and it may bite anyone who's been writing sloppy SQL if they upsize. Visual FoxPro returns a value, which is usually the last value it sees, but this is unreliable. If there are no aggregate fields, similar results may be obtained by using SELECT DISTINCT.

HAVING is used to filter the results after everything else (joins, filtering, and grouping) is done. If you want to filter on the results of a calculated field, HAVING is what you need, as you can see in this bit of code that finds duplicate key values:

```
SELECT KeyField, COUNT(*) AS NumRecords ;
  FROM MyTable ;
  INTO CURSOR Temp ;
  GROUP BY KeyField ;
  HAVING NumRecords > 1
```

SQL syntax for modifying data

We can modify data with INSERT-SQL, UPDATE-SQL, or DELETE-SQL. Unlike their Xbase cousins, these commands lock records when acting upon multiple records in a table, reducing contention problems at the cost of a little drop in performance. At the same time, they are more easily turned into SQL pass-through command strings or SQL stored procedures, in the event that the application is upsized to an SQL back-end database.

These commands are set-based—that is, they act on sets of data that meet a criterion, rather than affecting the immediate record the pointer is on. Consequently, when updating a single record, you'll always want to know the key value for the record in question. For modifying multiple records, you'll find the WHERE clause similar to the FOR clause in the corresponding Xbase command.

The UPDATE-SQL command supports subqueries, useful for changing values based on what exists in another table. Here's some code to show how it works:

```
*!* Give the customers who had large purchases a "preferred customer" discount
nPreferredCustomerDiscount = .15
UPDATE Customers ;
  SET Discount = nPreferredCustomerDiscount ;
  WHERE CustId IN ;
  (SELECT Orders.CustID ;
  FROM Orders ;
  WHERE Orders.OrderTotal >= 1000)
```

Locking, buffering, and transactions to prevent update conflicts

We need to begin planning our data update strategy by asking ourselves what should happen when two users want to edit the same data at the same time. We may want to allow both users to edit the data, and save their changes, letting the "last one win." We call this strategy "optimistic" because it optimistically assumes that conflicts will seldom occur, and that we will accept the outcome, whatever it is, if simultaneous edits occur. For complicated edits, or mission-critical data, use the "pessimistic" strategy of locking the record before the edits begin, and notifying other users that the record is currently in use. That way a second user will not begin long, complicated edits, only to have them lost or to find that the work has already been done.

Our strategy should also include a plan for letting the user back out of changes easily, which is usually done by storing a copy of the data in memory, and editing the copy, with the actual update taking place at the click of a Save button.

Finally, we need to allow for a way to make a group of changes to more than one table, and a way to back out of all of them cleanly if any part of the process fails. You can see why this is important when you consider online shopping. When inventory amounts change quickly, the customer may want to put a "hold" on some widgets, subtracting them from inventory, while his billing information is collected and approved, and the transaction is completed. If the credit approval falls through, the widgets need to be replaced in inventory (or never actually subtracted) to restore the system to its previous state.

We'll present an overview of locking, buffering, and transactions here, and encourage you to study Chapter 17 of the *Microsoft Visual FoxPro 6.0 Programmer's Guide*, "Programming for Shared Access," for the nitty-gritty of this complicated topic.

Buffering of tables

Buffering is a method of protecting updates to data in a multi-user environment where editing directly in the table would be a disaster! The "buffer" is a temporary holding area of memory that stores a copy of the data. The command to update from the buffer to the table is TABLEUPDATE(), and the command to wipe out changes in the buffer, should that be necessary, is TABLEREVERT(). We can either buffer a row at a time or hold changes for multiple records by buffering at the table level.

Buffering comes in two flavors, "pessimistic" and "optimistic." Pessimistic buffering locks the row or table while we perform our edits and updates, and then unlocks it, while optimistic buffering waits until we have finished our edits, and then locks, updates, and releases the locks. The updates themselves are done when the record pointer moves, for row buffering, or when TABLEUPDATE() is issued or the table closes, for table buffering. Care must be taken that the record pointer not be moved prematurely by some other part of the application if row buffering is in use; a private data session will help protect against this possibility.

Locking

When a user is about to undertake a time-consuming, complicated edit, we might want a way prevent other users from making similar edits and not being able to save their changes, or overwriting the first user's edits. We can specifically place a lock on a record as the user begins the edit, code to trap for "record in use" errors, and release it when we're done. We can also let Visual FoxPro do this for us by using pessimistic buffering, set with CURSORSETPROP(). The commands for manual locking are RLOCK(), FLOCK(), and UNLOCK().

This type of locking, placed before the actual edit and released when the edit is complete, is not available in views.

Buffering of views

Visual FoxPro automatically buffers views. We have a choice of buffering at the row level when the user is expected to edit and save one row of data in one table, or at the table level when the user is expected to edit several related rows in a group, and is expected to save the group as a whole. For example, you might use row buffering when changing a customer's master record (say, to update the telephone number). You'd probably use table buffering when adding or deleting items to an order the customer has placed, before giving him the invoice total amount. This would allow you to store the whole order at once.

Visual FoxPro actually locks the back-end record only momentarily while the data is written to the table, and this occurs when the view's record pointer is moved or the view is closed.

We don't have the opportunity to lock records ahead of time, as in pessimistic table buffering, but we can check for changes and ask the user what to do if the back-end value has changed during the edit process, as described later in the section "What if the record has changed?" Another approach is a specifically coded "semaphore" locking system where a record can be flagged as "not available" during an edit.

Transactions

Transactions allow us to package sets of related updates, and back out cleanly if needed. This is accomplished by wrapping the series of updates in a transaction, with the logic illustrated here:

```
BEGIN TRANSACTION
*!* Try to update the parent
IF TABLEUPDATE(0, .F., ParentTable)
  *!* Now try the child
  IF TABLEUPDATE(2, .F., ChildTable)
    END TRANSACTION
    WAIT WINDOW "Changes saved" NOWAIT TIMEOUT 1
  ELSE
    *!* Problem with child, but parent was already updated
    *!* Reverse the updates and notify the user
    ROLLBACK
    MESSAGEBOX("Problem updating the child table")
  ENDIF
ELSE
  *!* Problem updating the parent record
  *!* Reverse whatever we did and notify the user
  ROLLBACK
  MESSAGEBOX("Problem updating the parent table")
ENDIF
```

After we've ROLLBACKed a transaction, the back-end data is returned to its original state. This is not the case, however, for our copy of the data in the buffered view, where our pending changes are still visible. We can choose to try the transaction again, or discard our local changes with the TABLEREVERT() command.

Transactions are only available for views, and tables contained in a database; they are not available for Visual FoxPro free tables or FPW tables. To use transactions with non-database tables, access them through views.

What if the record has changed?

This seems to be the logical place to mention OLDVAL(), CURVAL(), GETFLDSTATE(), and GETNEXTMODIFIED(), all useful commands for determining whether the back-end data has changed during the course of a user's edit. Use these when attempting to prevent or resolve update conflicts.

Using GETNEXTMODIFIED(), you can see whether the user has changed any of the records in the view. Then you can loop through the fields in the record, using GETFLDSTATE() to see whether that particular field has changed. Then, use OLDVAL() to get the original back-end value to compare to CURVAL(), which retrieves its current value. If they're different, you can notify the user that the back-end data has changed since the process began and ask what to do. Here's how it looks:

```
*!* Get first modified record
nNextModified = GETNEXTMODIFIED(0)

*!* Loop through the buffer looking for changed data
DO WHILE nNextModified  <> 0
  GO nNextModified
  RLOCK()

  *!* Loop through the fields to find ones that have been changed
  FOR nFieldNumber = 1 to FCOUNT()
    IF GETFLDSTATE(nFieldNumber) = 2  && Field has changed by user

      *!* Check whether field has been changed by someone else
      *!* while this user was making edits
      IF OLDVAL(FIELD(nFieldNumber)) <> CURVAL(FIELD(nFieldNumber))

        *!* Field has been changed by someone else
        *!* Give user a choice how to proceed
        IF MESSAGEBOX("Value has changed, keep your edits?", 4) = 7  && "No"

          *!* User wants to back out of changes.
          *!* Revert record to current disk state.
          TABLEREVERT(.F)
          UNLOCK RECORD nNextModified

        ENDIF
      ENDIF
    ENDIF
  ENDFOR
  nNextModified = GETNEXTMODIFIED(nNextModified)   && Find the next record to do
ENDDO
TABLEUPDATE(.T., .T.)  && Force updates to all records
```

Stored procedure strategies for automatic actions

We can add program code to our database by putting it in stored procedures and calling it as an insert, update, or delete trigger. This code is always available and runs when triggered by the data, even if our data is accessed from outside Visual FoxPro or our application. We discuss stored procedures further in Chapter 8, "Creating a Physical Database," where we show how to create and maintain them, but our purpose at this stage of our application is to think of what actions we want to happen automatically when data is changed. These may be actions like cascading updates and deletes, which Visual FoxPro can help us with, or business-related things like an e-mail message sent to confirm an online sale when the sale record is committed.

To add a trigger, edit the database's stored procedures and code the function you want. Use the Table tab of the Table Designer and put the call to your function in one of the text boxes, as shown in **Figure 4**.

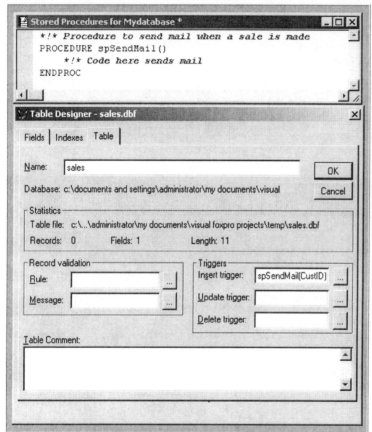

Figure 4. *Adding a stored procedure to send mail to the customer when a sale is made, and calling it with a trigger.*

Importing and exporting data

Besides creating a remote view and querying it or adding records to it, we can use the Visual FoxPro commands IMPORT, EXPORT, COPY TO, and APPEND FROM to move data in from or out to certain foreign file formats that Visual FoxPro natively supports. The file types supported are detailed in the Help and include import capability for Paradox, Lotus, and Excel files and append capability for some additional formats including delimited text files and System Data Format files. Capabilities for exporting data are similar.

IMPORT creates a new table from the foreign data, complete with Visual FoxPro's attempt at appropriate field names, while APPEND FROM requires an existing table or cursor to hold the new data. If records are appended from a .CSV file using the TYPE CSV syntax (new in

VFP6), the first record, containing field names, is ignored, while using the DELIMITED syntax with the comma-separated values file leaves one with the field names as an unwanted first record. APPEND FROM can also be used with Visual FoxPro data, where fields are matched by name, rather than assigning data to fields by the order in which they appear. To avoid bugs, remember that anything in the FOR clause of APPEND FROM is evaluated against the receiving table, not against the imported data.

Because COPY TO duplicates all of EXPORT's features, and adds some, you might bypass EXPORT and use COPY TO exclusively. COPY TO substitutes zeros and blanks for null values. Unusual formats can be created with syntax similar to:

```
COPY TO MyFile DELIMITED WITH "|" WITH CHARACTER "*"
```

This produces output similar to:

```
|Field1|*|Field2|*|Field3|
```

ADO, OLE DB, and RDS

ADO, or ActiveX Data Objects, is important to understand, because it's Microsoft's key strategy for accessing data. Microsoft's Universal Data Access is a great concept: data as an object that is accessible and behaves in much the same way no matter where it came from or who's talking to it, while exposing unique properties of the back-end data source. Microsoft has coupled its OLE DB providers, a group of lower-level components, with ADO, a set of high-level interfaces for working with data.

An important complement to ADO, especially for Web development, is Microsoft's Remote Data Services (RDS), a technology designed to cache data on the workstation and assist with marshalling, or moving data back and forth from the client to the server. Coupled with the fact that you can open and populate a disconnected ADO recordset object asynchronously, marshalling improves both actual and perceived performance because the client is free to do other things while data is being returned from the server.

If you think using a browser as a front end is the wave of the future, you'll quickly see how strategic these technologies are toward riding that wave. You can get ADO when you install the Microsoft Data Access Components (MDAC), either separately or as part of Internet Explorer, which is why IE sometimes needs to be installed for applications that don't appear to be browser-related.

Using ADO

Foundational to using ADO is the concept that there are more kinds of "data" than relational tables. One example of non-relational data is a document such as an e-mail message. ODBC, which was designed for relational data, does not have the capability to serve the e-mail message from the back end to the client, so Microsoft added a new technology, an OLE DB provider, to the toolbox and began developing OLE DB providers for the various types of databases and other sources of information such as the e-mail mentioned earlier. For those data stores that might not yet have their own OLE DB provider, there is a Microsoft OLE DB provider for ODBC.

There are four ADO objects you can use in your data access strategy:

- ADORecordset

- ADOConnection

- ADOCommand

- ADOError

You'll find that these correspond in concept to the SQL results cursor, SQLCONNECT(), SQLEXEC(), and the error messages returned, all building blocks you are accustomed to using. The ADO objects are not hierarchical, so you can create and use them in any order.

Connecting

To get the connection string for the back-end data store, use Notepad to create a file called MyLink.UDL. Double-click on MyLink.UDL and use the GUI interface to specify your database. Using Notepad again, open MyLink.UDL. The connection string is whatever is after the line that says, "Everything after this line is an OLE DB initstring."

Code for connecting to a database looks like this:

```
OConnection = CREATEOBJECT("AdoDB.Connection")
CConnectionString = [Provider = Microsoft.Jet.OLEDB.4.0; ] + ;
  [Data Source = C:\Documents and Settings\All Users\Application Data] + ;
  [\SBT\Databases\Northwind Traders Sample Company.mdb; ] + ;
  [Persist Security Info = False]
oConnection.Open(cConnectionString)
```

Using recordsets

There are four types of recordsets in ADO:

- Forward only—This recordset may be navigated in the forward direction only. You don't see changes to the data.

- Keyset—With this recordset, you'll see the changes when other users modify the data, but you won't see adds or deletes.

- Dynamic—You'll see all changes to the data with this recordset.

- Static—This recordset is a "snapshot" of the data and will not be updated in any way.

Like the objects we are familiar with in Visual FoxPro, ADO recordsets have properties and methods that we will use as we access the data they contain. Code for stepping through a recordset and examining its values looks like this:

```
*!* Assume we're already connected
*!* Retrieve some data and read through it, showing what it is
ORecordset = oConnection.Execute("SELECT * FROM Customers")
DO WHILE NOT oRecordSet.Eof
  FOR EACH oField IN oRecordSet.Fields
```

```
    ? oField.Name + ": " + oField.Value
  ENDFOR
  ORecordSet.MoveNext
ENDDO
```

Notice that there is no SCAN for a recordset. You can step through the recordset using the MoveNext method, though.

You'll find a detailed description of all the properties and methods of the ADO objects in John V. Petersen's article in the MSDN Library, "ADO Jumpstart for Microsoft Visual FoxPro Developers." You'll surely notice how much has been borrowed from Visual FoxPro for this trend-setting technology.

Sample Questions

You're designing an application that can use either native FoxPro tables or an SQL database as a back end. You handle your data selection by building an SQL statement and passing it to a function that knows which type of back end you're using, and returns a cursor with the data.

Assuming that zero-amount orders represent "no sale" transactions, which of the following will return customer information for customers who made purchases, for any back-end database? (Choose all that are true.)

A.

```
SELECT Customers.CustID, Customers.CustName, Customers.CustAddress, ;
  SUM(Orders.OrderAmount) AS OrderTotal ;
  FROM Customers INNER JOIN Orders ;
  ON Customers.CustID = Orders.CustID ;
  WHERE Orders.OrderAmount > 0 ;
  GROUP BY CustID
```

B.

```
SELECT Customers.CustID, Customers.CustName, Customers.CustAddress, ;
  SUM(Orders.OrderAmount) AS OrderTotal ;
  FROM Customers INNER JOIN Orders ;
  ON Customers.CustID = Orders.CustID ;
  WHERE Orders.OrderAmount > 0 ;
  GROUP BY Customers.CustID, Customers.CustName, Customers.CustAddress
```

C.

```
SELECT Customers.CustID, Customers.CustName, Customers.CustAddress, ;
  SUM(Orders.OrderAmount) AS OrderTotal ;
  FROM Customers ;
  WHERE Customers.CustID IN ;
  (SELECT CustID FROM Orders WHERE Orders.OrderAmount > 0) ;
  GROUP BY CustID
```

D.

```
SELECT Customers.CustID, Customers.CustName, Customers.CustAddress, ;
  SUM(Orders.OrderAmount) AS OrderTotal ;
  FROM Customers ;
  WHERE LOOKUP(Orders.OrderAmount, Customers.CustID, Orders.CustID) > 0 ;
  GROUP BY Customers.CustID, Customers.CustName, Customers.CustAddress
```

Answer: B only

You're designing a stock market application where shares and available dollars change quickly. You want to be able to mark the shares as sold, then get credit approval before subtracting the spent dollars from the customer's account and ending the transaction. If the transaction cannot be completed, you want to return the available dollars to spend and available shares to buy to their original states, as customers will often attempt the purchase again, this time purchasing fewer shares.
   Which of the following code outlines will accomplish this goal?

A.

```
BEGIN TRANSACTION
*!* Mark the shares as unavailable/sold
IF NOT TABLEUPDATE(...)
  ROLLBACK
ELSE
  *!* Subtract the cost of the sale from the account
  IF NOT TABLEUPDATE(...)
    ROLLBACK
  ELSE
    END TRANSACTION
  ENDIF
ENDIF
```

B.

```
BEGIN TRANSACTION
*!* Mark the shares as unavailable/sold
IF NOT TABLEUPDATE(...)
  ROLLBACK
ELSE
  *!* Subtract the cost of the sale from the account
  IF NOT TABLEUPDATE(...)
    ROLLBACK
  ELSE
    END TRANSACTION
    TABLEREVERT(...)
  ENDIF
ENDIF
```

C.

```
BEGIN TRANSACTION
*!* Mark the shares as unavailable/sold
IF NOT TABLEUPDATE(...)
  ROLLBACK
ELSE
  *!* Subtract the cost of the sale from the account
  IF NOT TABLEUPDATE(...)
    ROLLBACK
    TABLEREVERT("Account")
    TABLEREVERT("Shares")
  ELSE
    END TRANSACTION
  ENDIF
ENDIF
```

D.

```
BEGIN TRANSACTION
*!* Mark the shares as unavailable/sold
IF NOT TABLEUPDATE(...)
  ROLLBACK
  TABLEREVERT("Account")
ELSE
  *!* Subtract the cost of the sale from the account
  IF NOT TABLEUPDATE(...)
    ROLLBACK
    TABLEREVERT("Account")
    TABLEREVERT("Shares")
  ELSE
    END TRANSACTION
  ENDIF
ENDIF
```

Answer: D

Further reading

- "ADO Jumpstart for Microsoft Visual FoxPro Developers," John V. Petersen, MSDN Library Technical Articles

- "Data Buffering in Visual FoxPro," John Koziol, Visual FoxPro Articles, **www.universalthread.com**

- *Joe Celko's SQL For Smarties: Advanced SQL Programming, Second Edition*, Joe Celko

- *Microsoft Visual FoxPro 6.0 Programmer's Guide*, Chapter 17, "Programming for Shared Access"

- *Microsoft Visual FoxPro 6.0 Programmer's Guide*, Chapter 21, "Implementing a Client/Server Application"

- MSKB Q129889 "How to Use a UDF in Index with the Trim Functions"

- *Visual FoxPro 6 Enterprise Development*, Rod Paddock, John V. Petersen and Ron Talmage, Chapter 10, "Creating a Visual FoxPro Database"

Chapter 8
Creating a Physical Database

Data is the heart of our Visual FoxPro applications, and since we have a good logical design for our data, the physical database design falls easily into place. Let's look at the tools Visual FoxPro gives us for building and maintaining our database.

The characteristics of these tools, the Visual FoxPro tables and database container, come into play as we interpret our logical data model. In Visual FoxPro there are often many ways that any particular application can be designed, and our knowledge of these tools will help us choose the best solution with due regard to preserving data and referential integrity, enhancing performance, minimizing downtime and offering easy expansion as the customer's needs change.

Database and table design

Let's review the parts of the VFP database that we can use for housing our data, relationships and associated procedures, and the tools that VFP provides for us to create and maintain these databases. The elements of a Visual FoxPro database are:

- Tables
- Local views
- Remote views
- Stored procedures
- Persistent relationships
- Referential integrity
- Connections
- The database container

We can create and maintain each of these through the GUI interface, or programmatically in code. One helpful strategy is to create the database through the GUI interface, and then run the VFP utility program GenDBC.PRG to keep a record of what we've done. Let's discuss each of these elements of the database individually. We'll look at GenDBC.PRG and generated referential integrity code in the next section.

Tables

Tables are the backbone of our data store, with each row, or record, containing a group of data items, and the data items stored in columns or fields. Each field has a data type specified. There is usually a need to be able to access a particular record in our data, so we must allow for a way to do this by designating a field or group of fields as the primary key for our table, as discussed in Chapter 2, "The Logical Data Model."

Visual FoxPro tables come with additional features besides rows, columns, and indexes. They include support for null values, default values, field-level and record-level validation rules, and insert, update and delete triggers.

These capabilities allow us to program the database to do a lot of our work for us, rather than forcing us to code certain checks or responses every time a particular event happens in our database. These database-centered capabilities are especially helpful when the data may be accessed through many different channels.

Null support and default values

Null support and default values are complimentary features. In FoxPro 2.6 tables, it can be difficult to determine the difference between a value that is specifically entered as zero and a numeric field that has never been entered at all, or the difference between a value of SPACE(10) and no value at all in a character field. Allowing our fields to have null values solves this problem. In many cases, though, we do not want null values, and we want to be able to make a specific entry if no other value has been entered. For example, Visual FoxPro's support for default values allow us to enter the date and time and UserID of the person making the entry in every transaction by specifying these as default values for the tWhen and cWho fields in our tables.

Validation rules

Field-level and record-level validation rules in the database allow us to make the most basic checks on our data, and enforce these checks even when data is accessed from outside our applications. Imagine that a user wants to be able to connect to Visual FoxPro automobile insurance data through a program he has written in another language. Imagine also that there's a character field for the vehicle owner's gender in the Owners table, and only "M" or "F" is valid in this field. We don't want the user to be able to enter "X" or even "m" or "f." If we've added a rule to the field validation in the table to only accept "M" or "F," he won't be allowed to do this, even through an ODBC connection, and we won't have "dirty" data. In the old days of having all of the checks in our FoxPro code, we couldn't prevent these types of illegal values.

Field-level and record-level validation rules can be entered through the GUI interface of VFP's Table Designer. More importantly for this discussion, they can also be entered through the ALTER TABLE command, discussed later. Each rule should be an expression or function call to a stored procedure that will return a logical value. There is a mechanism provided to enter a message to show the user when the validation rule fails. The rules fire before leaving the field for a field-level rule and before the record pointer moves for a row-level rule. If the rule fails, the action (leaving the field or record) is prevented. When adding a new rule, we have the option to apply it to existing values or not.

An example of a row-level validation rule is checking the salutation field against the gender field. If the user entered "F" for the gender, the salutation might be required to be "Miss," "Mrs.," or "Ms.," but never "Mr." Again we benefit from the ability to add validation rules to our database that are applied to all data, whether the changes to it come from within our application or not.

We must remember what is appropriate to include in the field-level and row-level rules for our database, and when it might be more appropriate to include checks in business-tier objects. Values that can never be valid, like a birth date after today, should be in the field-level or row-level validation. Values that are valid for their field but may not be valid in the context of an application are better placed in the business objects of the middle tier. For example, consider insurance rates for "inexperienced" drivers. The age criteria for an inexperienced driver may change from time to time or from state to state. We might want to be able to override the usual application-level checks and enter a date of birth that would not be typical for an automobile owner at all. If the rules are not in the database itself, we can program around these rules when necessary. We can never program around the rule that a date of birth cannot be in the future, because we have put it in the database itself.

Insert, update, and delete triggers

Insert, update and delete triggers are actions that occur when data changes. They fire after the action occurs or when the record pointer moves. For example, when a user adds a new automobile owner to the Owners table, we might want to generate an invoice to be sent in the next mailing or add a callback entry to the agent's calendar to remind him in two weeks to verify that the new customer is happy with the service. When the status of a claim is changed to "Closed," we might want to send a notification e-mail to the agent and adjuster involved. When a vehicle is deleted from an account, we may want to calculate and send a refund of previous fees paid. The trigger calls can be entered through the GUI interface of the Table Designer or in code. The trigger code itself is in a stored procedure; because this is the way we can guarantee that it is always available to the database.

Local views

A view is a way to temporarily represent FoxPro data in a manner that may be structured differently than its source. We might create a view to show only a few particular records, to show denormalized data from more than one table, to provide an extra level of protection between the data the users are working with and the table itself so we can easily abandon changes, or to use Visual FoxPro features with legacy tables. Local views are views of FoxPro tables or views of FoxPro tables combined with remote data.

Remote views

A remote view offers the same features as a local view but usually has non-FoxPro data as its source and must include a reference to a database connection or a connection string. (Sometimes developers use remote views to connect to FoxPro data through ODBC to simulate client/server conditions.) We'll talk more about database connections in the "Connections" section later in this chapter. The remote database need only be available when we are defining the view at design time and when we open the view at run time.

Creating and maintaining views

Both local and remote views can be created through the VFP View Designer, though it has some limitations. Erik Moore's eView utility picks up where it leaves off. Once you've created the basic view in the View Designer, fire up eView to set the view properties visually or refine the SQL code, and generate a program that can then be used to create the new, more elaborate view. We discuss views again in the "CREATE SQL VIEW" section of this chapter and eView again in Chapter 11, "Maintaining and Supporting an Application."

Views can also be created completely in code by using the CREATE SQL VIEW command and using DBSetProp() for adjusting the view's properties. You can read more about these in the "CREATE SQL VIEW" and "DBSetProp()" sections later in this chapter.

Stored procedures

Stored procedures provide a vehicle for storing code with the data. This is ideal for procedures or functions that validate data or that run when data is inserted, updated or deleted. Stored procedures can be entered by using the "Edit Stored Procedures..." option on the shortcut menu of the Database Designer, through the Modify button of the Project Manager, by using MODIFY PROCEDURES from the Command window, or by using the APPEND PROCEDURES command to add code that is stored in another file. If the optional OVERWRITE keyword is omitted and there are two procedures with the same name, Visual FoxPro compiles and uses the one closer to the end of the file. If the OVERWRITE keyword is used, all procedures are overwritten, including any that are not being replaced. Use the APPEND PROCEDURES OVERWRITE command carefully!

Stored procedures offer an advantage over other program code in that they are loaded into memory when the database is opened and are therefore available at all times.

Persistent relationships

As described in Chapter 2, "The Logical Data Model," primary and foreign keys logically relate table entities. Here at the database level we use indexes on key fields, and relationships from index to index, to accomplish this objective. Though the vocabulary is similar, the concept of a persistent relationship is different from the relationships created with the SET RELATION command.

Persistent relationships aid in using the visual tools such as the Query and View Designers and the Data Environment Designer; allowing the tables to be joined automatically. They're also used by referential integrity enforcement code. It's possible to join a table to itself in a persistent relationship, allowing the definition of a relationship within a table for something like a licensed driver and the owner of the policy he's covered by, who is also in the table as a licensed driver.

We can establish persistent relationships through the GUI interface of the Database Designer by dragging the index key of one table to the index key of another. Relationships between primary or candidate indexes are by default one-to-one, and relationships between a primary or candidate index and a regular index are one-to-many. Many-to-many persistent relationships are not supported.

It's important to know that persistent relationships do not automatically relate tables opened in the Data Session window. In addition, relationships created in the Data Session window are lost when the data session closes, while persistent relationships persist, as their name signifies, with the database.

Referential integrity

Visual FoxPro provides a means to guarantee the integrity of foreign keys by allowing us to set up referential integrity rules. This means that we have a way to ensure that there are no orphan child records in the data when a parent record is removed from the parent table, and that we will not be allowed to create any orphan child records. The GUI mechanism to do this is the Referential Integrity Builder. It provides a choice of *cascade*, *restrict* or *ignore* rules for inserts, updates and deletes, and the code generated by the Referential Integrity Builder is kept with the other stored procedures in our database with a procedure name like "__RI_INSERT_MyTable." The procedures are called when the record pointer moves or TABLEUPDATE() is issued.

Visual FoxPro allows referential integrity rules for each persistent relationship in the database. By default, all referential integrity rules are set to *ignore* and no referential integrity code is generated. This means that nothing special happens when parent or child records change. Deciding what should happen when parent or child values change depends entirely on the needs of the customer. Orphaned child records may not be a problem for some customers!

Update and delete rules check for the presence of child records when the parent record is updated or deleted. *Restrict* prevents changes to the parent's primary key or deletion of the parent record if there are child records present. *Cascade* changes the foreign key of the parent in all of the child records when the parent record changes, and deletes all child records when a parent record is deleted.

Insert rules, on the other hand, check the parent when a child record is inserted or the value of the key field in the child record changes. The choices are *restrict* and *ignore*. *Restrict* prevents entering a foreign key value in the child table that does not occur in the parent table. This fact is not entirely obvious in the Referential Integrity Builder, but if you think about it, there's no sense in restricting the addition of new parent records to the parent table!

The Referential Integrity Builder does not allow us to do some more complicated types of checks, but we are always free to write our own routines. One commonly cited example is the case where the user should be prompted to re-assign the soon-to-be orphaned children to a different parent before the original parent is deleted.

Connections

Named connections in a database provide easy access to ODBC data, whether it is in a SQL database, a spreadsheet or another programming system like Microsoft Access. This means that the connection data is stored in one place, the database, and not in several places in the application. Having a named connection in the database allows us to optimize the connection settings. This is especially useful if the application accesses the remote database with a group permission and the users never know a login name or password for the back-end SQL database, or if we want to adjust the packet size or specify to disconnect when idle.

The database container

When FoxPro was reborn as Visual FoxPro and Microsoft added the new database objects discussed previously, the VFP team wanted to keep some level of backward compatibility with FoxPro 2.6 for the tables themselves. They accomplished this by adding the new features to a table called the database container and adding a link to the database container in the header of each table that belongs to a database.

To better understand the database container, it's worth looking at \FileSpec\60DBC.FRX and peeking inside a copy of the .DBC from TasTrade or one of your projects.

Programmatically creating and maintaining a database

Visual FoxPro comes with a wonderful utility, GenDBC.PRG, which can be run after setting up a database. It creates a program that can be used to learn how a database is created in code, to generate a database the first time our application is used, or to recreate a table if it becomes corrupt. Additionally, we can use the generated code as a model for doing things that are not easily done via the GUI interface.

Visual FoxPro's Referential Integrity Builder also generates code, which is stored with the database's stored procedures. The referential integrity code is generated each time we close the builder with the OK button. (To examine the current referential integrity settings without changing the code, use the Cancel button.)

In this section, we'll look at the code GenDBC generates, the commands that it uses and the code that the Referential Integrity Builder generates. We'll be using TestDatabase, shown in **Figure 1,** as our example. **Listing 1,** beginning on page 112, shows the GenDBC-generated code for TestDatabase. You can refer to it as we discuss the ways we can create and maintain a database. **Listing 2** (on page 117) has the stored procedures for TestDatabase, which include the spGetKey() function we have created and the procedures for the triggers, created by the Referential Integrity Builder.

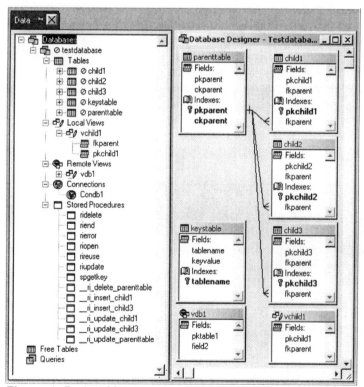

***Figure 1**. Project Manager and Database Designer views of TestDatabase, which contains tables, views, stored procedures, persistent relationships, referential integrity triggers and a connection.*

GenDBC.PRG

To paraphrase Robert Fulghum, "All I know about programmatically creating and maintaining Visual FoxPro databases, I learned from GenDBC." The GenDBC program is located in the \Tools\GenDBC folder, and the syntax to run it is:

```
DO GenDBC WITH MyGeneratedProgramName
```

GenDBC acts on the current database, and if the generated program name is not supplied, it allows you to choose a folder and supply a file name. We'll look at the following commands used by GenDBC in more detail:

- CREATE TABLE
- ALTER TABLE
- INDEX
- CREATE TRIGGER
- CREATE CONNECTION
- CREATE SQL VIEW
- DBSetProp()

CREATE TABLE

The CREATE TABLE command is at the heart building a database. We'll examine each of its keywords and clauses separately because there are many. Some keywords are used once and refer to the table as a whole, while others are used inside the parentheses that contain the field definitions and are potentially repeated for each field in the table. Much of the functionality of CREATE TABLE is repeated in the ALTER TABLE command.

FREE

Use the FREE keyword to signify that a table does not belong to the current database. You shouldn't see this keyword in GenDBC code, but it will be useful if you use some free tables in your application and you create all of your tables in code in a setup program that's run on the first use of your application.

NULL and NOT NULL

NULL and NOT NULL determine whether a field can have null values. If both are omitted, the current setting of SET NULL determines a field's ability to accept nulls, unless the field is indexed as a primary or candidate key, in which case it can never accept null values.

CHECK

When used within the field definitions, CHECK specifies that the next expression is a field-level validation rule with the text of the error message following the ERROR keyword in this clause. Be sure to use a user-friendly message!

Used apart from the field definitions, CHECK defines a row-level validation rule, and again is followed by an expression, the ERROR keyword, and the text of the error message.

DEFAULT
An expression for the default value for a field follows the DEFAULT keyword. Some developers prefer to never allow nulls or empty values in their data, using default values instead. In any case, the customer's needs usually dictate the use of nulls, empties or default values.

PRIMARY KEY and UNIQUE
The PRIMARY KEY and UNIQUE keywords specify that the field in question is a primary key or a candidate key and should therefore have only unique values. Notice that GenDBC does not use these keywords in its CREATE TABLE statement, but rather adds the indexes later with ALTER TABLE and INDEX. If we are hacking the code for our own purposes, this allows us to add data to the tables before adding the indexes, which can be a timesaver for really large files.

If the primary key or a candidate key is composed of more than one field, it can be defined outside the field definition parentheses using the PRIMARY KEY or UNIQUE clauses.

REFERENCES
If the current field is a foreign key, use the REFERENCES keyword inside the field definition parentheses to show a persistent relationship with the primary key of the parent table. If the foreign key is composed of something other than a single field, use FOREIGN KEY ... REFERENCES outside the field definitions.

Again, GenDBC adds foreign keys later on in the process with the ALTER TABLE command, allowing us more flexibility in using the generated code for other purposes.

NOCPTRANS
Finally, use the NOCPTRANS keyword to prevent translating character and memo fields to a different code page.

ALTER TABLE
ALTER TABLE is much like the CREATE TABLE command except that the table itself must exist before we start. Like CREATE TABLE, it has clauses that operate on the whole table and clauses that operate on a particular column. Of particular importance are the NOVALIDATE clause, which allows us to make changes without validating previously existing records against new field-level and row-level validation rules, and the SAVE keyword of the DROP FOREIGN KEY clause, which allows us to drop a persistent relationship with the parent table (added with the REFERENCES keyword) while keeping the index on the foreign key field in the current table. Primary indexes can only be specified with CREATE TABLE or ALTER TABLE (not with INDEX) because these commands add the information about the primary key to the database container.

INDEX

GenDBC does not create indexes in the CREATE TABLE statement. Instead, it adds them separately with ALTER TABLE and INDEX. As we mentioned earlier, this allows us to hack the code, appending data after the CREATE TABLE, and then index later.

Not surprisingly, INDEX creates indexes. A regular index is most commonly created with this syntax:

```
INDEX ON eExpression TAG TagName
```

There is no keyword for a primary index because it needs to be entered in the DBC. The CANDIDATE keyword will create a candidate index, with the requirement that all values in the field be unique. Confusingly, the UNIQUE keyword does not create a primary or candidate index. It only adds the first record with the indexed value to the index table, effectively hiding all other records. Imagine what happens when the indexed record is deleted, and you'll know why this misleading relic of the past should be avoided!

CREATE TRIGGER

As described earlier, triggers are actions that we want to perform when a record is inserted, updated or deleted, as well as a mechanism that can be used to preserve referential integrity. The code lives with the database, so we don't have to repeat code or function calls throughout our applications. The desired actions take place when changes occur, including cases where the data is accessed through the Command window or from outside Visual FoxPro. In general, the trigger code runs when the record pointer moves off of a record; a list of the commands that fire triggers, and exactly when they are fired, is included in Help.

Although GenDBC generates the CREATE TRIGGER commands for the database, the Referential Integrity Builder generates the code for the function that is called. Cindy finds it a good practice to not only generate the database code after each change, but also to save a copy of the generated referential integrity code in a .PRG file after each change.

The generated MakeRI function (near the end of Listing 1) sets up referential integrity. In the .DBC, Visual FoxPro uses a three-letter combination (with the first position for Update, the second for Delete, and the third for Insert, using "C" for *cascade*, "I" for *ignore*, and "R" for *restrict*) to record the referential integrity constraints. Code is generated only for relationships where at least one of the three is something other than *ignore*.

CREATE CONNECTION

We can programmatically create and store a connection to non-FoxPro data in our database with the CREATE CONNECTION command, which is pretty straightforward. The details are handled with DBSetProp() after the connection itself is created. For explanations of the properties, see Help for DBSetProp()'s inverse, DBGetProp().

CREATE SQL VIEW

Views are created programmatically with the CREATE SQL VIEW command. Creating a view entails putting three pieces together: the SQL SELECT statement, the details of the connection, and the properties of the view, set with DBSetProp(). We've discussed the details of the SQL language already in Chapter 7, "Creating Data Services," and we covered setting up a connection earlier in this chapter. We'll discuss DBGetProp() in depth in the next section.

We're left with a few keywords to discuss. Including the REMOTE keyword specifies that the view is a remote view. Visual FoxPro expects a connection to be named after the CONNECTION keyword and prompts for a connection or named data source if the connection name is not given. The SHARE keyword indicates that Visual FoxPro should use a shared connection if one is available. This is important if the remote server is licensed per connection, because the potentially costly alternative is for each view to have its own connection! Without the REMOTE keyword, the view is local.

DBSetProp()

DBSetProp(), and the related function DBGetProp(), are a little different from the CursorSetProp()/CursorGetProp() and SqlSetProp()/SqlGetProp() functions discussed in Chapter 7, "Creating Data Services," because they act on permanent properties of the database, rather than on temporary properties of something that's open.

These commands set or return properties for the database itself, its connections, fields, tables, and views. The properties vary in whether they are read-only or read-write. The best description of all of them is in Help under DBGetProp().

Listing 1. GenDBC.PRG generated code from our TestData database. If we run this code, we duplicate our database, minus the data.

```
* ************************************************************
* *
* * 2000/12/07     TestDatabase.DBC     08:48:30
* *
* ************************************************************
* *
* * Description:
* * This program was automatically generated by GENDBC
* * Version 2.26.67
* *
* ************************************************************

DisplayStatus([Creating database...])
CLOSE DATA ALL
CREATE DATABASE 'TestDatabase.DBC'
DisplayStatus([Creating table ParentTable...])
MakeTable_ParentTable()
DisplayStatus([Creating table Child2...])
MakeTable_Child2()
DisplayStatus([Creating table Child1...])
MakeTable_Child1()
DisplayStatus([Creating table Child3...])
MakeTable_Child3()
DisplayStatus([Creating connection conDb1...])
MakeConn_conDb1()
DisplayStatus([Creating view vChild1...])
MakeView_vChild1()
DisplayStatus([Creating view vDb1...])
MakeView_vDb1()
DisplayStatus([Creating persistent relations...])
```

```
MakeRelation_1()
MakeRelation_2()
MakeRelation_3()
DisplayStatus([Creating relational integrity rules...])
MakeRI()
DisplayStatus([Finished.])

***** Procedure Re-Creation *****
IF !FILE([TestDatabase.krt])
   ? [Warning! No Procedure File Found!]
ELSE
  CLOSE DATABASE
  USE 'TestDatabase.DBC'
  g_SetSafety = SET('SAFETY')
  SET SAFETY OFF
  LOCATE FOR Objectname = 'StoredProceduresSource'
  IF FOUND()
    APPEND MEMO Code FROM [TestDatabase.krt] OVERWRITE
    REPLACE Code WITH SUBSTR(Code, 70, 22184)
  ENDIF
  LOCATE FOR Objectname = 'StoredProceduresObject'
  IF FOUND()
    APPEND MEMO Code FROM [TestDatabase.krt] OVERWRITE
    REPLACE Code WITH SUBSTR(Code, 22254)
  ENDIF
    SET SAFETY &g_SetSafety
  USE
  OPEN DATABASE [TestDatabase.DBC]
ENDIF

FUNCTION MakeTable_ParentTable
***** Table setup for ParentTable *****
CREATE TABLE 'ParentTable.DBF' NAME 'ParentTable' ;
  (pkParent I NOT NULL DEFAULT spGetKey("ParentTable"), ;
  ckParent I NOT NULL)

***** Create each index for ParentTable *****
SET COLLATE TO 'MACHINE'
ALTER TABLE 'ParentTable' ;
  ADD PRIMARY KEY pkParent TAG pkParent
INDEX ON ckParent TAG ckParent CANDIDATE

***** Change properties for ParentTable *****
CREATE TRIGGER ON 'ParentTable' FOR DELETE ;
  AS __ri_delete_ParentTable()
CREATE TRIGGER ON 'ParentTable' FOR UPDATE ;
  AS __ri_update_ParentTable()
ENDFUNC

FUNCTION MakeTable_Child1
***** Table setup for Child1 *****
CREATE TABLE 'Child1.DBF' NAME 'Child1' ;
  (pkChild1 I NOT NULL DEFAULT spGetKey("Child1"), ;
  fkParent I NOT NULL CHECK BETWEEN(fkParent,1,100) ;
  ERROR "This is a field-level validation rule")

***** Create each index for Child1 *****
SET COLLATE TO 'MACHINE'
ALTER TABLE 'Child1' ADD PRIMARY KEY pkChild1 TAG pkChild1
```

```
INDEX ON fkParent TAG fkParent

***** Change properties for Child1 *****
CREATE TRIGGER ON 'Child1' FOR INSERT ;
  AS __ri_insert_Child1()
CREATE TRIGGER ON 'Child1' FOR UPDATE ;
  AS __ri_update_Child1()
ALTER TABLE 'Child1' ;
  SET CHECK BETWEEN(pkChild1,1,100) ;
  .AND. BETWEEN(fkParent,1,100) ;
  ERROR "This is a record-level validation rule"
ENDFUNC

FUNCTION MakeTable_Child2
***** Table setup for Child2 *****
CREATE TABLE 'Child2.DBF' NAME 'Child2' ;
  (pkChild2 I NOT NULL DEFAULT spGetKey("Child2"), ;
  sfkParent I NOT NULL)

***** Create each index for Child2 *****
SET COLLATE TO 'MACHINE'
ALTER TABLE 'Child2' ADD PRIMARY KEY pkChild2 TAG pkChild2
INDEX ON fkParent TAG fkParent

***** Change properties for Child2 *****
ENDFUNC

FUNCTION MakeTable_Child3
***** Table setup for Child3 *****
CREATE TABLE 'Child3.DBF' NAME 'Child3' ;
  (pkChild3 I NOT NULL DEFAULT spGetKey("Child3"), ;
  fkParent I NOT NULL)

***** Create each index for Child3 *****
SET COLLATE TO 'MACHINE'
ALTER TABLE 'Child3' ADD PRIMARY KEY pkChild3 TAG pkChild3
INDEX ON fkParent TAG fkParent

***** Change properties for Child3 *****
CREATE TRIGGER ON 'Child3' FOR INSERT ;
  AS __ri_insert_Child3()
CREATE TRIGGER ON 'Child3' FOR UPDATE ;
  AS __ri_update_Child3()
ENDFUNC

FUNCTION MakeConn_conDb1
***** Connection Definitions conDb1 *****

CREATE CONNECTION conDb1 ;
  DATASOURCE "MS Access Database" ;
  USERID "Admin" ;
  PASSWORD "Hello"

*****
DBSetProp('conDb1', 'Connection', 'Asynchronous', .F.)
DBSetProp('conDb1', 'Connection', 'BatchMode', .T.)
DBSetProp('conDb1', 'Connection', 'Comment', '')
DBSetProp('conDb1', 'Connection', 'DispLogin', 1)
DBSetProp('conDb1', 'Connection', 'ConnectTimeOut', 15)
```

```
DBSetProp('conDb1', 'Connection', 'DispWarnings', .F.)
DBSetProp('conDb1', 'Connection', 'IdleTimeOut', 0)
DBSetProp('conDb1', 'Connection', 'QueryTimeOut', 0)
DBSetProp('conDb1', 'Connection', 'Transactions', 1)
DBSetProp('conDb1', 'Connection', 'Database', 'db1')

ENDFUNC

FUNCTION MakeView_vChild1
***** View setup for vChild1 *****

CREATE SQL VIEW "vChild1" ;
  AS SELECT * FROM TestDatabase!Child1

DBSetProp('vChild1', 'View', 'UpdateType', 1)
DBSetProp('vChild1', 'View', 'WhereType', 3)
DBSetProp('vChild1', 'View', 'FetchMemo', .T.)
DBSetProp('vChild1', 'View', 'SendUpdates', .T.)
DBSetProp('vChild1', 'View', 'UseMemoSize', 255)
DBSetProp('vChild1', 'View', 'FetchSize', 100)
DBSetProp('vChild1', 'View', 'MaxRecords', -1)
DBSetProp('vChild1', 'View', 'Tables', 'TestDatabase!Child1')
DBSetProp('vChild1', 'View', 'Prepared', .F.)
DBSetProp('vChild1', 'View', 'CompareMemo', .T.)
DBSetProp('vChild1', 'View', 'FetchAsNeeded', .F.)
DBSetProp('vChild1', 'View', 'FetchSize', 100)
DBSetProp('vChild1', 'View', 'Comment', "")
DBSetProp('vChild1', 'View', 'BatchUpdateCount', 1)
DBSetProp('vChild1', 'View', 'ShareConnection', .F.)


*!* Field Level Properties for vChild1
* Props for the vChild1.pkChild1 field.
DBSetProp('vChild1.pkChild1', 'Field', 'KeyField', .T.)
DBSetProp('vChild1.pkChild1', 'Field', 'Updatable', .T.)
DBSetProp('vChild1.pkChild1', 'Field', 'UpdateName', ;
  'TestDatabase!Child1.pkChild1')
DBSetProp('vChild1.pkChild1', 'Field', 'DataType', "I")
* Props for the vChild1.fkParent field.
DBSetProp('vChild1.fkParent', 'Field', 'KeyField', .F.)
DBSetProp('vChild1.fkParent', 'Field', 'Updatable', .T.)
DBSetProp('vChild1.fkParent', 'Field', 'UpdateName', ;
  'TestDatabase!Child1.fkParent')
DBSetProp('vChild1.fkParent', 'Field', 'DataType', "I")
ENDFUNC

FUNCTION MakeView_vDb1
***** View setup for vDb1 *****

CREATE SQL VIEW "vDb1" ;
  REMOTE CONNECT "MS Access Database" ;
  AS SELECT * FROM Table1 Table1

DBSetProp('vDb1', 'View', 'UpdateType', 1)
DBSetProp('vDb1', 'View', 'WhereType', 3)
DBSetProp('vDb1', 'View', 'FetchMemo', .T.)
DBSetProp('vDb1', 'View', 'SendUpdates', .T.)
DBSetProp('vDb1', 'View', 'UseMemoSize', 255)
DBSetProp('vDb1', 'View', 'FetchSize', 100)
DBSetProp('vDb1', 'View', 'MaxRecords', -1)
```

```
DBSetProp('vDb1', 'View', 'Tables', 'Table1')
DBSetProp('vDb1', 'View', 'Prepared', .F.)
DBSetProp('vDb1', 'View', 'CompareMemo', .T.)
DBSetProp('vDb1', 'View', 'FetchAsNeeded', .F.)
DBSetProp('vDb1', 'View', 'FetchSize', 100)
DBSetProp('vDb1', 'View', 'Comment', "")
DBSetProp('vDb1', 'View', 'BatchUpdateCount', 1)
DBSetProp('vDb1', 'View', 'ShareConnection', .F.)

*!* Field Level Properties for vDb1
* Props for the vDb1.pktable1 field.
DBSetProp('vDb1.pktable1', 'Field', 'KeyField', .T.)
DBSetProp('vDb1.pktable1', 'Field', 'Updatable', .T.)
DBSetProp('vDb1.pktable1', 'Field', 'UpdateName', ;
  'Table1.pktable1')
DBSetProp('vDb1.pktable1', 'Field', 'DataType', "I")
* Props for the vDb1.field2 field.
DBSetProp('vDb1.field2', 'Field', 'KeyField', .F.)
DBSetProp('vDb1.field2', 'Field', 'Updatable', .T.)
DBSetProp('vDb1.field2', 'Field', 'UpdateName', ;
  'Table1.field2')
DBSetProp('vDb1.field2', 'Field', 'DataType', "C(50)")
ENDFUNC

***** Begin Relations Setup *****

FUNCTION MakeRelation_1
ALTER TABLE 'Child1' ADD FOREIGN KEY TAG fkParent ;
  REFERENCES ParentTable TAG pkParent
ENDFUNC

FUNCTION MakeRelation_2
ALTER TABLE 'Child2' ADD FOREIGN KEY TAG fkParent ;
  REFERENCES ParentTable TAG pkParent
ENDFUNC

FUNCTION MakeRelation_3
ALTER TABLE 'Child3' ADD FOREIGN KEY TAG fkParent ;
  REFERENCES ParentTable TAG pkParent
ENDFUNC

FUNCTION MakeRI
***** Referential Integrity Setup *****
CLOSE DATABASE
USE 'TestDatabase.DBC'
LOCATE FOR ObjectType = 'Table' AND ObjectName = 'Child1'
IF FOUND()
  nObjectID = ObjectID
  LOCATE FOR ObjectType = 'Relation' ;
    AND 'fkParent'$Property ;
    AND 'ParentTable'$Property ;
    AND 'pkParent'$Property ;
    AND ParentID = nObjectID
    IF FOUND()
      REPLACE RiInfo WITH 'CCR   '
    ELSE
      ? "Could not set RI Information."
    ENDIF
ENDIF
```

```
LOCATE FOR ObjectType = 'Table' AND ObjectName = 'Child3'
IF FOUND()
  nObjectID = ObjectID
  LOCATE FOR ObjectType = 'Relation' ;
    AND 'fkParent'$Property ;
    AND 'ParentTable'$Property ;
    AND 'pkParent'$Property ;
    AND ParentID = nObjectID
    IF FOUND()
      REPLACE RiInfo WITH 'RRR    '
    ELSE
      ? "Could not set RI Information."
    ENDIF
ENDIF
USE
ENDFUNC


FUNCTION DisplayStatus(lcMessage)
WAIT WINDOW NOWAIT lcMessage
ENDFUNC
```

Stored procedures and Referential Integrity Builder-generated code

The Referential Integrity Builder generates code each time it's closed with the OK button. The code is stored with the other stored procedures in the database. The stored procedure code for TestDatabase is shown in Listing 2.

First in the listing is our spGetKey() function for generating a primary key. We call this function to generate the default value for our key fields in tables Parent, Child1, Child2, and Child3. It serves as an example of a stored procedure we might add to a database.

Following our stored procedure is the generated referential integrity code. Note that it is carefully delimited with specially formatted header and footer comments that make it easy for the FoxPro engine to find and replace this code when the rules change. The code begins with the RiDelete, RiUpdate, RiError, RiOpen, RiEnd, and RiReuse procedures. These are used by the rule code itself to perform the necessary actions. Next come our rules. Each rule is named in the pattern __RI_INSERT_MyTable.

When regenerating the stored procedures by running the program generated by GenDBC, be sure to have the associated .KRT file in the same directory. The .KRT file contains the memo portions of the stored procedure records from the original .DBC.

Listing 2. *Stored procedure code from our TestData database. Our spGetKey() function is listed first, followed by the generated referential integrity code, which is too long to list here.*

```
FUNCTION spGetKey()
  LPARAMETERS pcKeyName
  LOCAL lnReturnValue, lnOldSelect

  lnReturnValue = 0
  lnOldSelect   = SELECT()
```

```
IF !USED("KeysTable")
  USE KeysTable SHARED IN 0
ENDIF

SELECT KeysTable
LOCATE FOR UPPER(ALLT(KeysTable.TableName)) ;
  = UPPER(ALLT(pcKeyName))
IF FOUND()
  DO WHILE NOT RLOCK()
  ENDDO
  lnReturnValue = KeysTable.KeyValue
  REPLACE KeysTable.KeyValue ;
    WITH KeysTable.KeyValue + 1 IN KeysTable
  UNLOCK
ELSE
  MESSAGEBOX("Bad key(" + pcKeyName + ;
    ") passed, call programming support. ")
ENDIF

SELECT (lnOldSelect)   && Restore work area
RETURN lnReturnValue

ENDFUNC

**__RI_HEADER!@ Do NOT REMOVE or MODIFY this line!!!! @!__RI_HEADER**

*!* About 700 lines of builder-generated code here

**__RI_FOOTER!@ Do NOT REMOVE or MODIFY this line!!!! @!__RI_FOOTER**
```

In *Effective Techniques for Application Development with Visual FoxPro 6.0*, Booth and Sawyer point out shortcomings of the generated code and include alternative referential integrity code. The important principle here is that wizards and builders have their limitations. We're always free to create our own builder, replace some of the functions, or start from scratch with our own code.

Database container maintenance

The .DBC table requires its own special maintenance processes. The VALIDATE DATABASE command performs consistency checks and can be used programmatically or in the Command window. When the database is open in shared mode, error messages are displayed only. With exclusive use, the .DBC's index is rebuilt as well. Include the RECOVER keyword, available from the Command window only, to invoke a repair mechanism that allows you to locate or delete missing items, or delete or rebuild problem indexes, provided that the appropriate information is available.

As we change objects in the database container, we leave behind deleted records related to those objects. The .DBC can be packed with the PACK DATABASE command. This command goes beyond the usual PACK command by renumbering the database objects, and PACK DATABASE—or its equivalent, Clean Up Database on the Database menu—is the only way a .DBC should be packed.

.DBC files are best stored with the data tables that belong to them. If all are moved together, problems are unlikely, but if they do not share the same directory and are moved around, difficulties with a table's backlink to the .DBC can be created. Freeing the table can cause problems if long field names are used. Fortunately, the link can be corrected with low-level file functions, as described in Chapter 7 of *1001 Things You Wanted to Know About Visual FoxPro* (Akins, Kramek and Schummer). Moving a .DBC has no effect on views.

Renaming a database container is also problematic, especially because its name is an integral part of view definitions. GenDBC comes in handy here because it allows us to capture the view definitions before we rename the database, rename the database, delete the bad views, change the old name to the new name in the view code, and recreate the views programmatically.

Normalization

We discussed normalization at great length in Chapter 2, "The Logical Data Model," when we discussed the logical model for the data. Now that we are actually creating the database, we need to review our final result against the normalization rules. We've moved from a platform-independent logical design to a platform-dependent physical design.

Are there reasons to denormalize? We might find a field that is seldom used and put it in a separate table, with a one-to-one relationship to its parent table. This allows us to leave this little-used data alone until we need it, providing us with a smaller, faster parent table. Another example is that we might find allowing a separate table for multiple contact addresses gives too little payoff when we have little use for the address data in the first place, and seldom have more than one per contact. We might have a calculated value that is used frequently and seldom changes, but is slow or otherwise difficult to arrive at. Our data might be part of a warehouse, conveniently summarized and ready to be retrieved for reporting purposes.

Denormalization is very data- and situation-dependent, and common sense should prevail. We also need to remember that "seldom" and "never" usually do happen!

Indexing strategies

Visual FoxPro's binary tree indexing strategy, known as the Rushmore technology, is one of the reasons for its incredible performance. An understanding of how to best take advantage of the Rushmore technology allows us to get the best performance from Visual FoxPro. Indexing can be done through the GUI interface of the Table Designer, or in code in a program or the Command window.

First, we must index our tables to support referential integrity, as discussed earlier. Indexing also speeds searching, sorting and filtering. The indexes we need to support referential integrity do double duty because we'll often be accessing data via our key fields. In general, we want indexes on the *exact expressions* used most often in the FOR, WHERE, or JOIN clauses of data access commands. We don't want to add more indexes than we need because each index adds a certain amount of overhead as records are added to, changed, or deleted in our tables.

Views can be indexed, but the index disappears when the view is closed. We can increase the speed of indexing a view if we USE MyView NODATA, apply the index and then fetch the data.

Some expressions can't be optimized

Chapter 15 of the *Microsoft Visual FoxPro 6.0 Programmer's Guide* describes the details of what is and isn't Rushmore-optimizable. A few things are noteworthy:

- Index expressions should exactly match the expression being compared. Index on UPPER(MyField) if you're going to be comparing in uppercase.

- Position the expression you're looking for on the left side of the of the equals sign.

- Commands with scope are optimized for ALL or REST but not for NEXT or RECORD.

- Commands that are "fully optimized" may or may not be faster than commands that aren't.

- Basic comparison operators—AND, OR, BETWEEN(), INLIST(), and ISNULL()— are optimizable; ISBLANK(), EMPTY(), and $ are not. A FOR or WHERE clause containing NOT is optimizable (if it would be optimizable without the NOT), but an index with NOT as part of the index expression can't be used for optimization.

- GO TOP and GO BOTTOM are not optimizable. LOCATE is.

- Rushmore does not use Index tags that are filtered, but Rushmore may be used in creating a filtered index.

- Use the machine collate sequence for indexes.

- Indexing on a field with only a few discrete values may not be a good idea if the data is on a network, including the often-mentioned index on DELETED().This is because FoxPro copies the indexes necessary for the data access command to the local machine, reads the indexes in order to determine which data to fetch, and then fetches the data. It then performs a final check on the retrieved data. For an expression that has only a few discrete values, it may be faster to perform the final check on a few retrieved records than to retrieve a large index in the first pass. Only a test with your data can help you decide what works best in your situation. If the data is on the local machine, index away!

Special considerations with indexing

FoxPro uses fixed-length indexes, so index values are always padded. This means that indexing on ALLTRIM(Name) does not gain any advantage. (Use SET EXACT OFF to SEEK a trimmed name.) Also, the very common expression UPPER(ALLTRIM(FirstName) + ALLTRIM(LastName)) leaves "Joe Lone" and "Joel One" looking like the same person. A much better idea is to keep the fields as they are and use any necessary padding to look for "JOE   LONE   " or "JOEL   ONE   ."

Finally, MSKB Q129889, "How to Use a UDF in Index with the Trim Functions," describes what happens when a user-defined function with internal trim commands is used as part of an index expression. In these cases, FoxPro makes several passes through the data in order to calculate the maximum width of the resulting field. The first two times, it ignores the trim functions in the UDF so it can determine the maximum width of the index expression. In the third pass, the trim functions in the UDF are applied. Finally, the result is padded to the (fixed) width of the index.

Sample Questions

You've asked your customer to specify a few details about how he wants things done and found out that he wants to always know whether or not data has been entered in a particular field in the Customers table, and that he wants all orders to have "Second day" shipping if not otherwise specified. All orders must have a link to a valid entry in the Customers table.

What must your database include to satisfy these needs?

A. Do not allow nulls in any fields in the Customers table, add a default value of "Second day" to Orders.ShipType, and add a referential integrity rule to cascade key changes from Customers to Orders and to restrict inserts in Orders.

B. Add a persistent relationship from Customers.CustID to Orders.CustID. Add default values of blank or zero to all fields in Customers. Add a row-level trigger to show a MessageBox to remind the users to be sure to enter "Second day" if they have no other shipping instructions, and to be sure to check that they have a valid CustID whenever they add a new order.

C. Allow nulls in all fields in the Customers table, add a default value of "Second day" to Orders.ShipType, and add a referential integrity rule to cascade key changes from Customers to Orders.

D. Add indexes on CustID in Customers and Orders. Add a persistent relationship between these tables based on the CustID field. Allow nulls in all fields except CustID in Customers. Add a default value of "Second day" to the Orders.ShipType field. Add a referential integrity rule that cascades changes from Customers to Orders and one that restricts inserts in Orders to valid CustID values.

Answer: D

You add thousands of new records to your main table each day and run your application with DELETED = ON. Your boss is considering having you add an index on DELETED() to the main table and asks you if this is a good idea.

Which of the following should you tell your boss, and why?

A. You tell her to add the index because it makes filtering out deleted records faster, and it's no extra overhead to add index records when the new records are added to the table.

B. You tell her to add the index because you saw a discussion on a newsgroup where some VFP guru said it was a good idea.

C. You don't necessarily want the index on DELETED() until you've tested under your own conditions. The DELETED() tag adds overhead when the new records are added, and you need to get a handle on the tradeoff between overhead and possible added speed in querying. You explain the tradeoffs and tell your boss that you'll need to do some testing with your particular data before giving a recommendation.

D. Both A and B.

Answer: C

Your application is used to print shipping labels twice a day for packages with the Rush field containing a value of .T. and OrderDate = DATE(). Your application runs with DELETED set ON.

Which of the following sets of tags for the Orders table is likely to give the fastest data selection, and why?

A. Index Orders on OrderDate and Rush, because they are the expressions used in the WHERE clause of the query.

B. Index Orders on OrderDate only, because it is used in the WHERE clause of the query. Though Rush is also used in the WHERE clause, and DELETED() is also included by implication, both of these have only a few discrete values. It is likely that there will be a speed advantage if the few records in the batch are examined on the local machine for their Rush and DELETED() values.

C. Index Orders on OrderDate, Rush, and DELETED(), because OrderDate and Rush are used in the WHERE clause of the query and because the application runs with SET DELETED ON.

Answer: B

Further reading

- *1001 Things You Wanted to Know About Visual FoxPro*, Marcia Akins, Andy Kramek and Rick Schummer, Chapter 7, "Working With Data"

- *Effective Techniques for Application Development with Visual FoxPro 6.0*, Jim Booth and Steve Sawyer, Chapter 4, "Data—Keys and Indexes"

- *Effective Techniques for Application Development with Visual FoxPro 6.0*, Jim Booth and Steve Sawyer, Chapter 6, "Rules, Triggers, and Referential Integrity"

- *The Fundamentals: Building Visual Studio Applications on a Visual FoxPro 6.0 Foundation*, Whil Hentzen, Chapter 3, "The Interactive Data Engine"

- *Microsoft Visual FoxPro 6.0 Programmer's Guide*, Chapter 6, "Creating Databases"

- *Microsoft Visual FoxPro 6.0 Programmer's Guide*, Chapter 7, "Working with Tables"

- *Microsoft Visual FoxPro 6.0 Programmer's Guide*, Chapter 8, "Creating Views"

- *Microsoft Visual FoxPro 6.0 Programmer's Guide*, Chapter 15, "Optimizing Applications," section on "Using Rushmore to Speed Data Access"

- MSKB Q129889 "How to Use a UDF in Index with the Trim Functions"

- "Performance Tuning Tips in Microsoft Visual FoxPro," Erik Svenson, Program Manager, Internet Tools and Platforms Division, Microsoft Corporation, MSDN Library Technical Articles

- *Visual FoxPro 6 Enterprise Development*, Rod Paddock, John V. Petersen and Ron Talmage, Chapter 10, "Creating a Visual FoxPro Database"

Third-party software

- eView by Erik Moore, #971, Visual FoxPro Downloads, **www.universalthread.com**, Public domain, .APP without source code

- Stonefield Systems Group: Stonefield Database Toolkit, provides full data dictionary support including changing table structures, rebuilding views, and adding or rebuilding indexes, **www.stonefield.com**

Chapter 9
Testing and Debugging
the Solution

You should test your code in small pieces as you develop it, making sure that buttons work or parameterized views show the appropriate selection of records, for example. You also want to test the application as a whole, to make sure it meets the customer's specifications. You need a way to make sure that each part is appropriately tested, and that environmental requirements such as response times are met. Finally, you want to ensure that the application satisfies the customer's specifications and, beyond that, his unspoken business needs. When the customer asks for revisions, you want to make sure that the revisions don't break any existing code, with the least amount of effort spent re-testing.

Testing is really an art in itself. It requires a systematic plan as well as the ability to anticipate every odd thing a user might try. You'll need your sharp eyes to catch any odd behaviors, or deviations from standards. There is also an art to preparing test data in such a way as to expose any errors in the program logic. It's easy to create data that will show that an application works under normal circumstances; it's very difficult to create data that will expose weaknesses you hadn't thought of in the first place!

Testing

As developers code their applications, they usually do quick tests to catch typing errors or to try out tricky statements. However, a more formal and thorough testing process is needed before code is released. This process should include the following types of tests:

- Unit testing

- Regression testing

- Integration testing

- Stress testing

- Beta testing

The object of testing is to make the application fail, so the test plan must include normal conditions, where the application is expected to perform correctly, to show that it does not fail; and abnormal conditions, where the application might be expected to perform incorrectly, to show that it handles these situations gracefully, or actually fails. We'll discuss each type of testing individually.

Unit testing

Unit testing, also called module or element testing, consists of testing individual processes or programs. Unit testing includes testing for things like division by zero, data type mismatches such as entering characters in a numeric field, entering unexpected characters such as symbols (+, *, -), entering non-printing characters such as CHR(0) or Tab, entering boundary values of a range such as the day before, day of, and day after the endpoints of a date range, and entering a negative number where only positive numbers are expected.

You should test forms at different screen resolutions and color settings to make sure they're readable, and test reports to make sure there is room enough for large numbers such as the grand total, and that everything continues to work when a different type of printer is used. You should test opening a file when the directory or file does not exist and when there are spaces in the file or directory names. You should test that a multi-user system can accommodate more than one simultaneous user.

Regression testing

As you do your unit testing, you're developing a standard battery of tests through which to run your application. Each time you make changes to existing modules, you'll want to re-run these tests to make sure you haven't broken anything that was formerly working. This process is called *regression testing*.

Regression testing is made easier by keeping a set of test data available, and having a written test plan so you know exactly which tests to perform. You should revise your test plan as you go along so you spend less time re-testing for bugs that have been corrected, though you need to re-test them occasionally to make sure that none of them reappear.

Finally, regression testing is made easier by Automation. With automated testing software, you can record a series of inputs for your program that become a script you can replay. Text from DEBUGOUT statements in your application, screen shots, and Coverage Profiler output can be compared against the results of a known good run. We'll discuss different ways that Visual FoxPro provides for capturing and analyzing some of this output as we move through this chapter.

Integration testing

As sections of an application are finished, they should be tested together, a process called *integration testing*. This phase of testing covers things like ensuring that data and variables are passed correctly between one module and the next, and that processes don't compete for record locks. You should also verify that the private data sessions are behaving correctly: that is, that the record pointers in the base tables and in copies of the tables in other data sessions are not affected by moving the record pointers of tables in the data session you are testing.

Stress testing

Stress testing means testing an application at the limits of its abilities. You should test with huge amounts of data, many users, unusual speed, and bursts of activity. Unless you have intended to prevent it, you should test what happens when more than one instance of your application is running.

The application's integrity may degrade when memory or CPU cycles are shared between its modules or with outside applications, so you should be sure to test in an environment where the user's usual concurrent applications, such as an e-mail client, browser, instant messaging, text processor, and media player, are running.

We often see minimum requirements for applications listed, and you should realize that these may not be the actual minimum conditions, but merely the minimum conditions for which the software provider has tested the application and guaranteed its functionality.

A good example of the need for stress testing is the well-known "fast processor" problem that occurs when FoxPro for Windows is run on today's faster machines. This older software shows problems when run at processor speeds unknown at the time it was originally developed.

Beta testing

The final phase of testing, where users test the application, is called *Beta testing*. (It's called "Beta" testing because the internal tests are seen as the "Alpha," or first, tests.) The Beta testers use the application in the same way they would if they were doing actual work, and provide feedback to the developer. Be sure to warn the Beta testers that there may be hidden problems and that mission-critical activities should not rely on the Beta version of the software. Beta testers should be provided with incentives to do thorough testing, and means to provide the types of feedback you will need to correct errors or make improvements.

Beta testers can be expected, through their general use of the application, to stumble upon issues that programmers never considered, providing suggestions to improve usability and discovering areas where the application may meet the stated specifications but not meet the customer's actual business needs.

Making sure you have tested all of the code

An important part of ensuring the quality of the applications you develop is thorough testing, and an important part of thorough testing is making sure every line of code was executed properly. In addition, it's often useful to know which sections of code take the most time, so efforts to optimize code can be leveraged against the benefits they will produce. Visual FoxPro's built-in logging function, combined with its Coverage Profiler is the right tools for these jobs. The logging function provides a line-by-line log of program activity, and the Coverage Profiler provides a summary of this log file in a more digestible format. While the logging function is built into Visual FoxPro, if you find the Coverage Profiler inadequate, you're free to write your own programs to digest the log file it creates.

You'll get the best use out of the coverage tools by configuring them properly. Begin by setting up a log file, most easily done via the Command window with SET COVERAGE TO MyLog.LOG [ADDITIVE]. The alternative is to open the Debugger and use the Toggle Coverage Logging button on the Debugger toolbar or the Coverage Logging item on the Debugger's Tools menu. Once you've specified a log, programs are automatically logged to it until you toggle Coverage Logging off. Use the ADDITIVE keyword if you want to append new data to the log, but be warned that this file can grow large very quickly. Logging produces a text file with one line for each command executed. The data on each line is comma-separated. Each line consists of the following:

- Time for executing the line

- Name of the class executing the code

- Object, method, or procedure containing the code

- Line number

- Full path and file name of code being executed

- Call stack level

Consider this little program:

```
*!* TestCoverage.PRG
A = 1
FOR i = 1 TO 5
  IF A = 1
    WAIT WINDOW "Do this line" TIMEOUT 1 NOWAIT
    IF i >= 3
      WAIT WINDOW "Then do this line" NOWAIT
    ELSE
      WAIT WINDOW "Sometimes do this line" NOWAIT
    ENDIF
  ELSE
    WAIT WINDOW "Never do this line"
  ENDIF
ENDFOR
```

Here's the coverage log produced by running the program:

```
0.008510,,testcoverage,1,d:\temp\testcoverage.fxp,1
0.000149,,testcoverage,2,d:\temp\testcoverage.fxp,1
0.000306,,testcoverage,3,d:\temp\testcoverage.fxp,1
0.005025,,testcoverage,5,d:\temp\testcoverage.fxp,1
0.000217,,testcoverage,6,d:\temp\testcoverage.fxp,1
0.001662,,testcoverage,9,d:\temp\testcoverage.fxp,1
0.000228,,testcoverage,10,d:\temp\testcoverage.fxp,1
0.094810,,testcoverage,11,d:\temp\testcoverage.fxp,1
0.000388,,testcoverage,14,d:\temp\testcoverage.fxp,1
0.000386,,testcoverage,3,d:\temp\testcoverage.fxp,1
0.002733,,testcoverage,5,d:\temp\testcoverage.fxp,1
0.084372,,testcoverage,6,d:\temp\testcoverage.fxp,1
0.001728,,testcoverage,9,d:\temp\testcoverage.fxp,1
0.000227,,testcoverage,10,d:\temp\testcoverage.fxp,1
0.000471,,testcoverage,11,d:\temp\testcoverage.fxp,1
0.000193,,testcoverage,14,d:\temp\testcoverage.fxp,1
0.000231,,testcoverage,3,d:\temp\testcoverage.fxp,1
0.001674,,testcoverage,5,d:\temp\testcoverage.fxp,1
0.000115,,testcoverage,6,d:\temp\testcoverage.fxp,1
0.001409,,testcoverage,7,d:\temp\testcoverage.fxp,1
0.000112,,testcoverage,8,d:\temp\testcoverage.fxp,1
0.000106,,testcoverage,11,d:\temp\testcoverage.fxp,1
0.000107,,testcoverage,14,d:\temp\testcoverage.fxp,1
```

```
0.000184,,testcoverage,3,d:\temp\testcoverage.fxp,1
0.001926,,testcoverage,5,d:\temp\testcoverage.fxp,1
0.000116,,testcoverage,6,d:\temp\testcoverage.fxp,1
0.001458,,testcoverage,7,d:\temp\testcoverage.fxp,1
0.000111,,testcoverage,8,d:\temp\testcoverage.fxp,1
0.000109,,testcoverage,11,d:\temp\testcoverage.fxp,1
0.000110,,testcoverage,14,d:\temp\testcoverage.fxp,1
0.000115,,testcoverage,3,d:\temp\testcoverage.fxp,1
0.002710,,testcoverage,5,d:\temp\testcoverage.fxp,1
0.000244,,testcoverage,6,d:\temp\testcoverage.fxp,1
0.001411,,testcoverage,7,d:\temp\testcoverage.fxp,1
0.000234,,testcoverage,8,d:\temp\testcoverage.fxp,1
0.000253,,testcoverage,11,d:\temp\testcoverage.fxp,1
0.086916,,testcoverage,14,d:\temp\testcoverage.fxp,1
```

You can see that the raw log is too unwieldy to use as a tool for program testing, so after you've run your test and produced a log file, use the Coverage Profiler to create a nice digest of the log. You can run the Profiler from the Tools menu or by typing this in the Command window:

```
DO (_COVERAGE) [WITH "MyLog.LOG"]
```

One thing you might want to adjust is the "Coverage marks" because the default pipe character (|) may not draw your eye to unexecuted lines. Cindy has set her coverage marks to "Exec" and "Not Exec," as shown in **Figure 1**. The Coverage Profiler allows you to refresh the display after changing the coverage marks, so you can experiment until you find what works best for you. It's worth noting that if you open the Profiler while you still have logging enabled, it just uses the open log. If logging is not enabled, you're prompted for the name of the log file (unless you've called the Profiler programmatically and specified a log file as a parameter).

The Coverage Profiler has two modes: Coverage (shown in Figure 1), which is the best view for examining whether particular areas of the code were executed, and Profile, which is for viewing the execution statistics.

The Coverage Profiler is a great tool, and time spent learning to get the most out of it is well spent, but if you find that you need something it just doesn't do, you can expand on or customize the source code (included with Visual FoxPro) to change either the way it compiles the statistics or the way it presents them. Instruct Visual FoxPro to use your new code by changing the value of the system variable _COVERAGE.

You can also call an add-in such as Markus Egger's Coverage Snippet Analyzer AddIn by using the Add-Ins button on the Coverage Profiler's toolbar and locating the desired file. Egger's add-in uses syntax coloring and bold fonts to call attention to code that is used often or is slow.

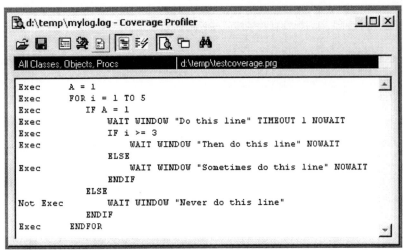

Figure 1. *Set the coverage marks so that your eyes are drawn to code that has not been executed.*

Testing every line

In your unit testing, you'll want to include actions and values that test every line of code. Make sure your test plan includes ways to make sure all of your "ELSE" code is executed, including entering various types of bad data such as no data at all, ridiculous values such as purchasing -1 widgets, mismatched data types such as "two" widgets, taking the wrong route through the application, and letting the cat walk across the keyboard. **Figure 2** shows the Coverage Profiler's Statistics dialog, which summarizes coverage and lets us know whether we've successfully tested every branch of code.

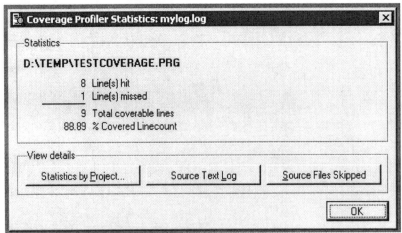

Figure 2. *It's easy to check whether there are any unexecuted branches of the code using this dialog from the Coverage Profiler.*

Finding where things get slow

Users love speed, and Visual FoxPro's speed is one of its selling points. Some speed requirements are only satisfied by good design, so you'll want to test your prototype early in the game. One time-consuming operation in Visual FoxPro is opening tables. We always have tradeoffs between opening and closing our tables each time we use them, which might be considered a more modular approach to application development, or opening tables at the beginning of the main program and keeping them open until the application closes. A little forethought at design time allows either or both of these approaches to be used, but without the forethought in the design stage, the developer may be locked into a poor, time-consuming way of handling the situation.

You'll want to spend your development time where it will reap the most benefits, so look through the Coverage Profiler's Profile output, shown in **Figure 3**, for the areas of code that are executed the most, and spend some of your code optimization time there. Shaving microseconds from a loop that is iterated millions of times can really add up to a lot of time saved.

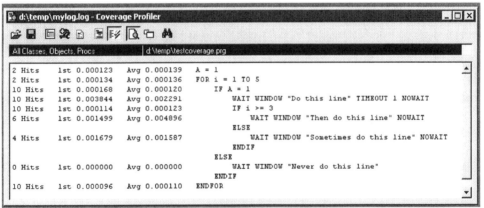

Figure 3. *The Coverage Profiler summarizes many lines of an execution log into a useful report that helps us decide where to spend our optimizing time.*

You may also want to look at areas of the code that take the most time and evaluate the tradeoffs of optimizing seldom-used code. Remember also that tricky, complicated code is harder to maintain than a slower, but more easily understandable approach, and there's probably little value in optimizing something that requires 15 minutes once a year!

While we're on the subject of code speed, if a slow-executing area of code involves a query or opening a view, use SYS(3054, 1) to check the optimization level of the SQL and SYS(3054, 11) to check for the efficiency of the joins. While we discussed indexing for optimization previously in Chapter 8, "Creating a Physical Database," we'd like to reiterate the fact that code that is partially optimized, as reported by SYS(3054, 1), may in fact be faster than code that is fully optimized. If DELETED is ON, SYS(3054, 1) will only show full optimization when a tag on DELETED() is included, yet tags with only a few discrete values can slow data selection down when there are not many deleted records in the table. Only testing under normal operating conditions can determine whether the use of such an index has a beneficial or detrimental effect on speed, and due to memory caching issues, the computer should be turned off between tests.

Code bugs you'll encounter

Unless you write perfect code (we'd like to meet you!), you'll find some code bugs during the testing process. The first plan of attack is always to prevent problems, but if they do occur we want to be able to find them. We'll talk here about the common types of bugs we encounter and how we can use the available tools to prevent them, and in the next section we'll talk about using Visual FoxPro's Debugger to help find any that have found their way into our code.

Typos

First off, typos plague all of us. We're either rotten typists, or we type too fast and make speed errors. A couple of features of the FoxPro editor can help here. If we camel-case each variable name carefully the first time we use it (that is, use mixed case to make it appear just as we want it), Beautify will take care of all other occurrences. Those that aren't properly "cameled" may have been typed incorrectly.

The Visual FoxPro program editor's syntax coloring offers some configuration choices that can really help with debugging. Syntax coloring helps with typos in command names. When FoxPro commands are set to show in the default blue (or any other color that's different from other items), the second word of "WAIT WINDOE" will be the wrong color, catching our attention as we type! If we apply back-color highlighting to our strings, typing the closing matching quote will add the highlighting, where a missing or mismatched single or double quotation mark won't, and we'll notice it for sure!

When compiling MyProgram.PRG, hit "Ignore all" if the error dialog pops up and then MODIFY FILE MyProgram.ERR to see or print a list of all the errors at one time. The Build option in the Project Manager gives you a similar list for all code in the project.

When piecing together SQL pass-through commands, using square brackets helps eliminate problems caused by strings with internal apostrophes or quotation marks. To catch problems caused by missing spaces, issuing `STRTOFILE(MyString, "Temp.TXT")` is the easiest way to see what you're actually passing to the server, and the lack of formatting sometimes helps in spotting other typos.

Run-time errors

Visual FoxPro can only alert you to run-time errors when the code is actually running, but these errors are usually easy to spot. If the Debugger is open, it's usually pretty easy to see actual values when a "Data type mismatch" error occurs, and it's easy to step back to a calling program to see why a variable wasn't passed correctly. We'll talk more about using the Debugger in the section "Debugging tools and techniques" later in this chapter.

Logic errors

Logic errors are far more difficult to spot, and their sources are more difficult to find. When testing, be sure to have sufficient test data available. Knowing exactly what data you have put in and what results you should have is essential, so you'll need to compute expected formula results by hand apart from the program code. If you can't create test data, find a way to work with a small subset of the data such as a week's worth of orders instead of a whole month, or only customers whose names begin with "B" so that you can cross-check your program code by using a calculator to calculate the exact totals and averages you should have in your result set. If you can create test data, be sure to create data that covers every possible combination of false and true values, for example.

For help tracking down logic errors, try explaining the situation to someone else. Cindy often finds that by the time she has adequately explained her problem for posting to a newsgroup or list, the answer becomes apparent. She's also used Truth Tables, stepping through code with a pencil and evaluating the variables, and "sleeping on" the problem as a means to debug difficult code.

Design errors

Poor application design sets the stage for errors down the road. If tables are not properly normalized—for example, having computed fields—special care needs to be taken to recompute those values every place in the application where their source data changes. A new coder coming along to make a program change might not be aware of such a constraint!

Another source of potential errors is the use of FoxPro reserved words, especially in table names or field names. While FoxPro is flexible and forgiving, why take a chance? The GUI Table Designer will never alert you to a problem name, but you can easily see how creating tables in code, with help from the editor's syntax coloring, will alert you quickly if you use reserved words as you design your tables.

Debugging tools and techniques

The Visual FoxPro Debugger is an essential tool for pinpointing the source of the types of bugs we mentioned earlier, and knowing how to use it efficiently is an essential part of your developer skill set. We're always mystified when we encounter newsgroup questions where the poster seems never to have tried using this useful tool to debug his code problem. Nearly all of us can benefit from learning to use it more efficiently.

The Visual FoxPro Debugger consists of the following windows:

- Trace

- Call Stack

- Locals

- Watch

- Debug Output

These windows are available either in the main Visual FoxPro window or in the Debugger, but all must be used the same way at any particular time. Activate these windows programmatically with the `ACTIVATE WINDOW` command. One of the main reasons for using the Debugger mode is that the configuration of the breakpoints and watched values can be saved and reloaded. Another reason, especially on a small monitor, is that the Debugger won't occupy screen space needed by the application itself. For developers with more screen real estate, using each window as it is needed, within the Visual FoxPro window, can be a good choice.

The Debugger allows you to customize each window's font individually, and each window may be docked or not. Docking the windows in the Debug frame lets you size all of the windows by sizing the frame, a useful feature, while docking the windows in the FoxPro frame seems awkward. Spend some time with each format to see what works best for you, and be prepared to change your approach as you move from one project to another.

Follow the flow with Trace and Call Stack

There's no substitute for stepping through code when there are difficult bugs to pinpoint. The Trace window, a familiar tool to most developers, shows each line of code as it executes, allows breakpoints to be set, and in general lets you know where you are. The Call Stack window completes the picture, allowing you to move forward and backward through levels of code, and giving you a more complete picture of program flow. When in the VFP development environment, SET STEP ON in any part of any code will bring up the Trace window and suspend execution.

Trace

Let's get to know the Trace window first. Two combo boxes, Object and Procedure, are only available when running code within an object. They allow you to find and examine code anywhere within the object hierarchy. Use the Object combo to access the object you want to see, and use the Procedure combo to see any method of that object that has code written for it.

The Trace window has a right-click menu that corresponds to most of the Debugger's toolbar buttons, and of course, all these items are in the Debugger's menu, too. Each of the menu options has a corresponding hot key combination so your mouse hand won't get overused. You can Open a program to load it into the Debugger, Resume program execution, Step Into code line-by-line, Step Over the tracing of a called procedure (though the procedure will be executed), or Step Out of a procedure if you've seen enough and want to speedily move to the calling procedure (again, the procedure will be completely executed).

The Set Next Statement option on the menu (there is not a corresponding toolbar button) is used to specify the next statement to execute. Use this option when you need to move back a few code lines, reset the value of a variable in the Locals window, and try the code again, or use this to jump ahead and skip some code entirely! To set the next statement, position the cursor on the line of code in the Trace window on the next line of code you want to execute. Then choose "Set next statement" from the right-click menu or the Debugger menu, and you're off! Lastly, use the Run To Cursor menu choice like a temporary breakpoint that won't have to be deleted later. Just position the cursor on the line you're aiming for in the code, choose Run To Cursor from the menu, and you're off! The program will execute to the marked line where it will stop in Step mode, waiting for a further prompt from you.

Finally, use Do to start a program running from within the Debugger, Throttle to determine how fast Visual FoxPro will execute code, and best of all, if you're in the Debug frame, use Fix to fix code. This time-saving option cancels program execution and brings up the program editor with the desired line of code highlighted, ready for your changes. If your Locals window isn't large enough to show all variables, simply hold the mouse cursor over a variable in the Trace window to see its current value in a ToolTip.

Call Stack

The Call Stack window shows the route taken through the application code to get to the current location in the program. If you're having trouble with something like passed parameters, you can move back through the program levels in the Call Stack by clicking a different level, causing the Trace, Watch, and Locals windows to show the program environment for that level of the code, and check the passed parameters as they were just before moving to the next code level. Then you can move forward again to the executing section of code to see whether anything was lost in the transition. This offers an excellent way to catch variable scoping problems.

Canceling program execution

There are several ways to cancel program execution. Choose the Cancel button on the toolbar (red dot), Debug | Cancel from the Debugger's menu, or type CANCEL in the Command window. If there is an error, a Cancel option may be available from the error dialog also.

Check or change values with Locals and Watch

All variables and objects are shown in the Locals window when they are in scope, but variables, objects, and expressions are only shown in the Watch window when you add them there. You can set breakpoints on entries in the Watch window to catch when they change— for example, a variable goes out of scope, the currently selected work area changes, the record pointer changes in a table, and so on. Add an expression to the Watch window by typing it in, dragging it from the Command window, or dragging it from the Trace or Locals window. You can even drag a Watched expression back into the text box and edit it to add a similar expression. Extremely useful!

While the Locals window automatically shows current variables so you don't have to add them all to the Watch window, you can't set breakpoints on their values from within the Locals window. You can change the visibility status of different types of variables using the context menu. The Public and Local choices show only those variables specifically declared as PUBLIC or LOCAL, the Standard view shows everything in scope, and the Objects choice toggles the visibility of object references.

One of the best features of Locals and Watch is that you can use them to change values! Have you come to an area of the program you need to step through but the value of some important variable is incorrect? Have you stepped through several repetitions of a loop and still need one more time through to pinpoint what is going wrong? Just select the value in either Locals or Watch, change it, and continue on in your program. The possibilities here are endless.

Reporting progress with Debug Output

The Debug Output window shows the results of DEBUGOUT statements and event tracking, which we'll describe further in "LISA G and understanding events." All of the things we used to put in WAIT WINDOWs can be sent to the Debug Output window, with the added benefit of not needing to convert values to character data types, and a more permanent record of the output messages! Even more important, DEBUGOUTs don't interfere with program flow the way WAIT WINDOWs and MESSAGEBOXes do. It's hard to find some timing-related issues when these are used as debugging aids.

DEBUGOUT statements can send code to the Debug Output window only in development mode when the window is active, so there is no need to worry about the presence of these commands in shipped executables.

Stop and see what's happening with breakpoints

Breakpoints stop program execution. You can see what is happening in a particular section of code as it executes, check on the values of variables, or possibly even change their values. Breakpoints can be set in the Trace or Watch windows by double-clicking the left margin, or they can be set with the Breakpoint dialog, available through the menu and the Debugging toolbar. A third way to set a breakpoint is to right-click in the program editor and choose Set Breakpoint. Be aware that the "Clear all breakpoints" toolbar button deletes breakpoints, rather than disabling them as is an option in the Breakpoint dialog.

Breakpoints can be set on a line of code, stopping execution *before* the line, or on an expression, stopping execution *after* the line of code that caused the expression to become true.

Breakpoints only fire when the Debugger is running, but do not require the Trace window itself. To save time, use the Debugger in the Debug Frame with no windows open. Your breakpoints will fire, and you can trace just the sections of code you need to see.

Alerting yourself to abnormal conditions with ASSERT

The ASSERT command allows you to specify a condition that you expect to be true, and a message to show if it is not. As you can see in **Figure 4**, it's really an inline way of combining an IF statement and a MESSAGEBOX, with the added capability of easily turning all evaluations and messages off. If you don't want the speed loss that comes with evaluating them, issue the SET ASSERTS OFF command. ASSERTs are not evaluated at all with the run-time version, though the ASSERT statements remain in the code.

Figure 4. ASSERT alerts you if the expected condition is not met. You can use the system-generated default message, or specify one of your own.

LISA G and understanding events

Two of the common errors made by new developers are misunderstanding the difference between events and the execution of object methods that these events trigger, and misunderstanding the order of events when a form instantiates. This results in situations like trying to check the value of a control that has not yet instantiated. Make friends with LISA G, Drew Speedie's events girl, who reminds us that form method code is called in the following order: Load, Init, Show, Activate, and GotFocus, and spend some time instantiating complex forms with Event Tracking turned on. Understand that events happen and methods are called when they happen. Consequently, if there is code in the Click() method of your command button that calls a user-defined method, MyClick(), you will see the Click event in the Event Tracker but no reference to MyClick(). Finally, be careful which events you track. MouseMove and Paint will fill up the window very quickly with useless information, and the events you want to see will be quickly lost. We suggest you stick with tracking the more useful events like Activate, Click, Deactivate, Error, GotFocus, Init, InteractiveChange, KeyPress, Load, LostFocus, QueryUnload, Valid, and When, and then add any other particular event that is giving trouble.

In Visual FoxPro, container objects such as forms, containers, pageframes, commandgroups, and the like instantiate "from the inside out." That is, the innermost controls are instantiated, then their parent container, and then that container's parent container, until finally the form itself instantiates. **Figure 5** shows the results of turning event tracking on and instantiating a form. Since the Event Tracker does not display the Show() method, we forced it with a DEBUGOUT statement.

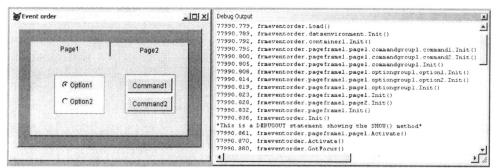

Figure 5*. We've tracked the events that occurred when instantiating a form. Notice how the Init methods for the container controls Container1 (shaded), PageFrame1, OptionGroup1, and CommandGroup1 are executed "from the inside out," within the LISA G event order of frmEventOrder itself.*

Developers often make the mistake of assuming that code in the Init() method of a form will already have executed when the Init for the form's controls runs. After all, when we create a form, we make the form first, and then add controls to it, right? To illustrate how this works, we've added a property to our form in the Init() method, and added a PEMSTATUS() call to the Init() method of each control on our form to see whether the form property is available at each of those points. Here's what we copied out of the Debug Output window:

```
frmeventorder.Load()
frmeventorder.dataenvironment.Init()
frmeventorder.container1.Init()
Property not available
frmeventorder.pageframe1.page1.commandgroup1.command1.Init()
Property not available
frmeventorder.pageframe1.page1.commandgroup1.command2.Init()
Property not available
frmeventorder.pageframe1.page1.commandgroup1.Init()
Property not available
frmeventorder.pageframe1.page1.optiongroup1.option1.Init()
```

```
Property not available
frmeventorder.pageframe1.page1.optiongroup1.option2.Init()
Property not available
frmeventorder.pageframe1.page1.optiongroup1.Init()
Property not available
frmeventorder.pageframe1.page1.Init()
Property not available
frmeventorder.pageframe1.page2.Init()
Property not available
frmeventorder.pageframe1.Init()
Property not available
frmeventorder.Init()
The next line of code adds the property.
Property available
The property was added in the Init method.
*This is a DEBUGOUT statement showing the SHOW() method*
frmeventorder.pageframe1.page1.Activate()
frmeventorder.Activate()
frmeventorder.GotFocus()
```

The Bring to Front and Send to Back menu items change the order of instantiation, with controls in back instantiating first, as shown in **Figure 6**.

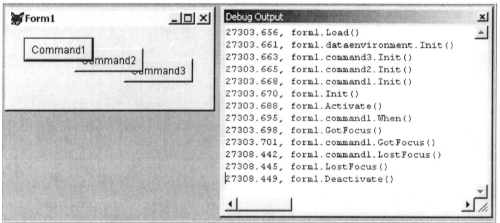

Figure 6. Controls in back are instantiated before those in front of them.

Error handling

Many developers handle errors with a global routine set with ON ERROR soon after the application starts. These routines usually trap for and recover from a few anticipated errors and handle the rest by notifying the user with some sort of canned message and closing up shop.

When you move from this simple approach to error handling to routines that are customized to meet the specific needs of the objects they are associated with, you begin to understand that error handling follows the hierarchy of the class and not the hierarchy of the container. This means that if an error occurs in a text box on a form and the text box control has no specific error method, Visual FoxPro looks for error-handling code in the text box's parent class, and then in objects on the call stack, and finally in the ON ERROR routine if there is one. Finally, Visual FoxPro does its own error handling, which basically means that the application has crashed. Visual FoxPro does not look for error-handling code in the container hierarchy (the form the control is on) unless specifically instructed to do so. If the developer wants to call error code in the parent container object instead of in the control's parent class, each control should have This.Parent.Error() or ThisForm.Error() in its error method.

Debugging code and application distribution

Our efforts to test and debug our code may leave us with bloated applications that are full of odd WAIT WINDOWs or other messages that we don't want the users to see. There are things we can do to prevent or eliminate these types of problems as we build and distribute our finished product. As usual, there are tradeoffs for some of the choices we will need to make.

Visual FoxPro lets us choose whether to include source code information when we build our applications. The "Debug info" check box in the Project Information dialog and the NODEBUG keyword of the COMPILE command determine whether the information is included or not. Without the debugging information, error reports may be difficult to use, and the small amount of size reduction in the executable may not be a worthwhile trade.

The preprocessor commands #If, #IfDef, and #IfNDef, together with #EndIf allow us to conditionally add or remove code from the executable file as it is compiled. Judicious use of these commands can result in smaller, faster applications, while providing full debugging capabilities at design and test time. #If tests to see whether a particular condition is true, #IfDef tests whether a variable is defined, and #IfNDef tests whether a variable is not defined—all direct the compiler to include or exclude the code between them and the #EndIf, depending on the results. These provide the perfect way for us to turn debugging code such as MESSAGEBOXes or WAIT WINDOWs on and off, without requiring us to remove them before the application ships. After a short look at these exciting commands, you'll see lots of uses for them!

If we have code that may run under several different Visual FoxPro versions, we can use the VERSION() function to determine which we are running and what service packs may have been applied. Wrapping code inside an IF statement that checks VERSION(4) allows us to use new commands that may only be available in a service pack without breaking code for users who do not have the service pack applied, and checking the return value of VERSION(3) allows us to see the language for which Visual FoxPro has been localized.

VERSION(2) allows us to see whether we're running in development or run-time mode, but querying the Visual FoxPro application object for it's StartMode property goes even further. **Table 1** shows the values returned by _VFP.StartMode in various circumstances.

Table 1. *Values returned by _VFP.StartMode.*

Value	Description
0	Visual FoxPro was started as an interactive session.
1	Visual FoxPro was started through the instantiation of an application object; for example, through a command like: `oMyObject = CREATEOBJECT("VisualFoxPro.Application")`
2	Visual FoxPro was started as an out-of-process Automation server.
3	Visual FoxPro was started as in in-process .DLL Automation server.
4	Visual FoxPro was started as a distributable .APP or .EXE.

Wrapping debugging code inside a check for the circumstances under which Visual FoxPro is running can be extremely useful. During development of a COM server, you will definitely want to test the code interactively and receive visible feedback from the application, but when the COM server is in production it should have no interactive interface. By wrapping error-handling code inside a check of _VFP.StartMode, you can more easily test and debug code that will eventually be built and released as a COM server, without having to remove any interactive debugging capabilities or resort to COMRETURNERROR() as the only means of obtaining debugging information.

Special debugging issues with COM servers

Prior to VFP6, VFP Automation servers couldn't properly return error conditions to their callers. Now, we can use the COMRETURNERROR() function to populate the COM exception structure with error information and return control to the client, which can determine how to proceed. The COM server remains in memory and execution continues with the next method that is called by the client. In the Error() method of the COM server, the developer can determine what actually occurred, populate the Source parameter with the source of the error, and populate the Description with anything needed to describe the error. The Description parameter allows reporting of the same error number and error text that we are accustomed to having when we troubleshoot our executable code, and the client can be programmed to deal with that information locally. Other choices for handling errors from within COM servers include things like writing to an error log or sending a notifying e-mail.

The SYS(2335) function is another improvement in VFP6. It allows the Unattended Server Mode for out-of-process COM servers to be turned on and off. If a COM object is instantiated on an unattended server and produces an error, there is usually no one to notice the message box and respond to it, leaving the client waiting and not knowing what went wrong. If the COM server is instantiated locally, any message box that appears may be hidden behind a form and not seen, again, disabling the machine.

By checking the StartMode property, issuing a SYS(2335, 0) as soon as possible after a COM server is instantiated, and trapping for any errors that might produce a modal state, the developer can eliminate problems when COM servers need to run on unattended machines.

Sample Questions

Your customer wants you to squeeze every possible bit of speed out of an application written by another developer. He provides you with source code, funds you for a week of work, and says that the speed of the data entry module annoys his users the most.

How do you spend your time?

A. You print out the code and begin reading, looking for sloppy code, and spend your time fixing all the capitalization in the variable names.

B. You ask for details of a typical data entry scenario. You step through the application with Coverage Logging running. You look for both lines of code with the greatest execution time and lines of code that are executed the largest number of times, and then spend the rest of your time trying to optimize those particular lines of code.

C. You ask for details of a typical data entry scenario. You step through the application with Coverage Logging running. You look for lines of code with the greatest execution time and spend the rest of your time trying to optimize those particular lines of code.

D. You ask for details of a typical data entry scenario. You step through the application with Coverage Logging running. You look for lines of code that are executed the largest number of times and spend the rest of your time trying to optimize those particular lines of code.

Answer: B

You're having a problem when a form instantiates. You assign the name of a .WAV file containing a short greeting to a form property in the Init() method, and you want to play the .WAV file at some point before the form gets focus.

Where can you put the code to play the .WAV file?

A. In the Init() method after the form property is assigned, or in the Show() or Activate() methods.

B. In either of the Show(), or Activate() methods.

C. In the Init() method after the form property is assigned, or in the Load() or SetFocus() methods.

D. In any of the Load(), Show(), or Click() methods.

Answer: A

You need overall departmental totals for 20 divisional budgets, and you've decided that writing a program to do this through OLE Automation of Excel is a better approach than trying to type all the formulas into Excel directly. Some text for the budget categories is in columns 1-7, departmental totals for six different categories (for which you need formulas) belong in columns 8-13, and the individual divisions that you need to total are 20 groups of six columns, beginning in column 14. Rows 1-4 have header information, and the budget amounts are in rows 5-57. You have the following code:

```
WITH oExcel.Sheets("MySheet")
  FOR lnRows = 5 TO 57
    FOR lnCols = 1 TO 6
      lcFormulaR1C1 = ""
      FOR lnDivs = 1 TO 20
        *!* Build a formula that is the sum of the 20 Divisional cells
        lcFormulaR1C1 = lcFormulaR1C1 + "," + ;
          "R" + ALLT(STR(lnRows)) + "C" + ALLT(STR(7 + lnDivs * lnCols))
        *!* Strip off the leading comma and put the formula in the cell
```

```
         .Cells(lnRows, 7 + lnCols).FormulaR1C1 = ;
           "= SUM(" + SUBSTR(lcFormulaR1C1, 2) + ")"
       ENDFOR
     ENDFOR
   ENDFOR
ENDWITH
```

The code gives

```
"= SUM(R5C8,R5C9,R5C10,R5C11,R5C12,R5C13, ...)"
```

as the formula for the first cell, but you know it should be

```
"= SUM(R5C14,R5C20,R5C26,R5C32,R5C38,R5C44,...)"
```

Which of the following will give the desired formula?

A.

```
WITH oExcel.Sheets("My Sheet")
  FOR lnRows = 5 TO 57
    FOR lnCols = 1 TO 6
      lcFormulaR1C1 = ""
      FOR lnDivs = 1 TO 20
        *!* Build a formula that is the sum of the 20 Divisional cells
        lcFormulaR1C1 = lcFormulaR1C1 + "," + ;
          "R" + ALLT(STR(lnRows)) + ;
          "C" + ALLT(STR(7 + lnCols + (6 * lnDivs)))
        *!* Strip off the leading comma and put the formula in the cell
        .Cells(lnRows, 7 + lnCols).FormulaR1C1 = ;
          "= SUM(" + SUBSTR(lcFormulaR1C1, 2) + ")"
      ENDFOR
    ENDFOR
  ENDFOR
ENDWITH
```

B.

```
WITH oExcel.Sheets("My Sheet")
  FOR lnRows = 5 TO 57
    FOR lnCols = 1 TO 6
      lcFormulaR1C1 = ""
      FOR lnDivs = 1 TO 20
        *!* Build a formula that is the sum of the 20 Divisional cells
        lcFormulaR1C1 = lcFormulaR1C1 + "," + ;
          "R" + ALLT(STR(lnRows)) + ;
          "C" + ALLT(STR(7 + 6 + lnDivs * lnCols))
        *!* Strip off the leading comma and put the formula in the cell
        .Cells(lnRows, 7 + lnCols).FormulaR1C1 = ;
          "= SUM(" + SUBSTR(lcFormulaR1C1, 2) + ")"
      ENDFOR
    ENDFOR
  ENDFOR
ENDWITH
```

C.

```
WITH oExcel
  .Sheets("My Sheet").SELECT()
  FOR lnRows = 5 TO 57
    FOR lnCols = 1 TO 6
      lcFormulaR1C1 = ""
      FOR lnDivs = 1 TO 20
        *!* Build a formula that is the sum of the 20 Divisional cells
        lcFormulaR1C1 = lcFormulaR1C1 + "," + ;
          "R" + ALLT(STR(lnRows)) + ;
          "C" + ALLT(STR(7 + 6 * lnDivs + lnCols))
        *!* Strip off the leading comma and put the formula in the cell
        .Cells(lnRows, 7 + lnCols).FormulaR1C1 = ;
          "= SUM(" + SUBSTR(lcFormulaR1C1, 2) + ")"
      ENDFOR
    ENDFOR
  ENDFOR
ENDWITH
```

Answer: A

Further reading

- *1001 Things You Wanted to Know About Visual FoxPro,* Marcia Akins, Andy Kramek and Rick Schummer, Chapter 13, "Miscellaneous Things"

- "Automate Your Testing," Manfred Rätzmann, *FoxPro Advisor*, December 1999

- *The Fundamentals: Building Visual Studio Applications on a Visual FoxPro Foundation,* Whil Hentzen, Chapter 19, "Using the Debugger;"

- *The Fundamentals: Building Visual Studio Applications on a Visual FoxPro Foundation,* Whil Hentzen, Chapter 21, "The Coverage Profiler"

- *Hacker's Guide to Visual FoxPro 6.0,* Tamar Granor and Ted Roche, "#Define, #UnDef, #If, #EndIf, #IfDef, #IfNDef, #Include, _Include"

- *Hacker's Guide to Visual FoxPro 6.0,* Tamar Granor and Ted Roche, "Productive Debugging"

- "HOWTO: Use COMRETURNERROR() Function in an OLE Server," MSDN Library, Q187908, **http://support.microsoft.com/support/kb/articles/Q187/9/08.ASP**

- *Microsoft Visual FoxPro 6.0 Programmer's Guide,* Chapter 4, "Understanding the Event Model"

- *Microsoft Visual FoxPro 6.0 Programmer's Guide,* Chapter 14, "Testing and Debugging Applications"

- *Microsoft Visual FoxPro 6.0 Programmer's Guide,* Chapter 32, "Application Development and Developer Productivity"

- *Testing Computer Software, Second Edition*, Cem Kaner, Jack Falk and Hung Quoc Nguyen

- "Vfpcom.exe Using COM Language Enhancements in VFP 6.0" (article and downloadable example), MSDN Library, Q188709, **http://support.microsoft.com/support/kb/articles/Q188/7/09.ASP**

- "Visual FoxPro Coverage Profiler Add-Ins and Subclasses," Lisa Slater Nicholls, MSDN Library Technical Articles, **http://msdn.microsoft.com/library/techart/vfpcover.htm**

Third-party software

- ErrHandler Forum, hosted by Mike Asherman, extensive code, articles, and discussion, **www.ideaxchg.com/ix07/er/_sys/toccontu.htm**

- "Error Handling in Visual FoxPro," Doug Hennig, includes article and extensive code for handling errors during execution, **www.stonefield.com/pub/errorh.zip**

- Markus Egger's Coverage Snippet Analyzer AddIn, **www.eps-software.com/isapi/eps.dll?Products~DSC+Markus+Egger's+Coverage+Snippet+Analyzer+AddIn**, .APP file with accompanying article, "Using Markus Egger's Coverage Snippet Analyzer Addin"

Chapter 10
Deploying an Application

An application isn't complete until it's installed. The Setup Wizard lets you prepare various installation media, and it handles issues of registering COM/DCOM components. For some applications, you also need to set up clients and servers for remote Automation and Microsoft Transaction Server (MTS).

Like many developers, you probably put little thought or effort into deploying applications. At best, it is a rushed process the night before deployment. Bottom line, deployment takes a very small portion of the life cycle of an application, but nevertheless it is a crucial element of a successful application.

Setup Wizard

We won't cover the setup wizard screen by screen, but instead will focus on the portions highlighted by the Microsoft outline and items that developers have difficulty with. Chapters 13, 25, and 26 from the *Microsoft Visual FoxPro 6.0 Programmer's Guide* cover compilation and the Setup Wizard in detail.

In Step 2 of the Setup Wizard (see **Figure 1**), the "COM components..." check box brings up a typical add/remove list (see **Figure 2**) where the components can be included. The interesting part is the "Install remote COM components" check box. This tells the setup routine to automatically register the remote components. Selecting a COM component and clicking the Details button allows you to specify the server details and the nature of the component (COM, remote Automation or DCOM).

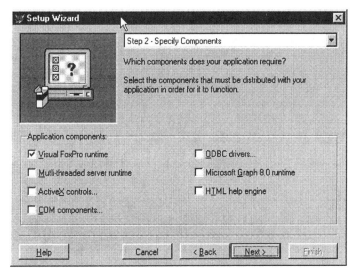

Figure 1. The components that can be included in a setup.

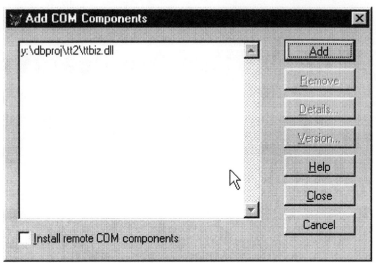

Figure 2. The Add COM Components list box from Step 2 of the Setup Wizard.

Only check "Multi-threaded server runtime" (shown in Figure 1) if you have compiled your application with this option, because it replaces VFPR.DLL (the normal VFP runtime) with VFPT.DLL. A multi-threaded .DLL allows several requests to be processed at once. With a single-threaded .DLL, a request must finish before the next one can start.

In Step 3 of the Setup Wizard (see **Figure 3**), you choose the folder where your setup files will go. The 1.44MB option breaks the install image into several folders smaller than 1.44MB. This allows the files to be easily copied onto a floppy disk. Websetup compresses the installation files and puts them into one folder. As the name implies, this makes the installation smaller and therefore easier to download over a slow Web connection. Netsetup is identical to Websetup except that it is not compressed. This makes it larger, but it will execute faster. If your installation will be from a CD, you can use either of the last two options. If the application is large, you may need to choose the Websetup type. In our experience, the compression appears to reduce the size of an installation image by about 50 percent.

Step 4 of the Setup Wizard (see **Figure 4**) lets you specify a post-setup executable. This is a program that runs after the setup routine finishes. It can be used to launch another setup routine, bring up a registration screen, display a ReadMe file, or perform other tasks that the Setup Wizard can't do natively. The post-setup executable does not need to be an .EXE file; it can also be a batch file. The batch file can then call other files such as VBScript via the Windows Scripting Host (WSH).

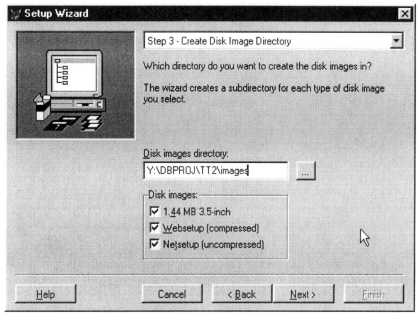

Figure 3. All three disk image types selected.

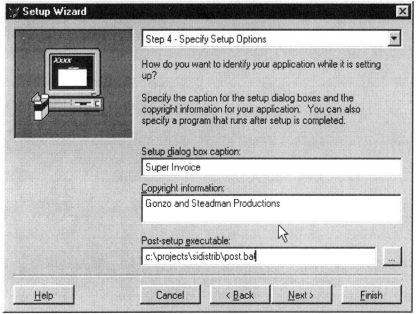

Figure 4. Step 4 of the Setup Wizard showing a batch file as the post-setup executable.

> The Setup Wizard can't create a desktop shortcut inherently. See MSKB Q238553 for information on creating a post-setup executable to do this, or MSKB Q244677 for information about how to use WSH.

> If the post-setup executable is written in VFP, the VFP runtime must already be installed on the client computer. This is an important restriction if you are installing VFP for the first time because the VFP runtime isn't available until after an OS reboot. In this case, you can use WSH or an .EXE that either doesn't need a runtime (C++ or Delphi) or that already has its runtime installed.

In Step 7 (see **Figure 5**), you can choose to "Generate a web executable file," which further compresses the setup into one file called WEBAPP.EXE, making it quicker and easier to download and run from the Web. The .EXE is put into the directory that you specified in Step 2, not the Websetup directory. Note that with a Web executable, you lose the ability to do a quiet install. We'll discuss this further in the next section.

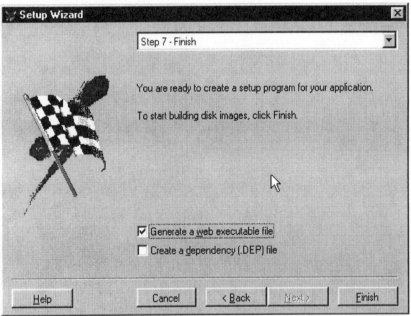

Figure 5. *Step 7 of the Setup Wizard showing the selection to "Generate a web executable file."*

Installing the application

Applications are often deployed by double-clicking on the SETUP.EXE that has been generated from the wizard. There are several command line switches that help make deployment go more smoothly. You can get a list of switches by typing SETUP / at a DOS prompt.

> SETUP / causes a dialog box to be displayed indicating error 530. Click the OK button and you'll see the command line option descriptions.

The command line switches, especially /Q, allow you to deploy updates via login scripts and maintain control of where and how the application is installed. The available switches are shown in **Table 1**.

Table 1. The available command line switches.

Switch	Description
/A	As far as we can tell, the /A switch isn't valid in Visual FoxPro. We get an error when we use it, and the Visual FoxPro documentation does not explain it.
/G filename	Creates a text file that contains the details of the installation, including: time stamps of all activity, registry keys modified, files copied, dialog box details, operating system and more. By default this file goes into the Windows Temp directory.
/Q0	Does not display any choices for the user. Only a progress bar is displayed while the installation is running, and upon completion, a message is displayed showing whether or not the application has been installed successfully.
/Q1	Same as /Q0, except the final dialog is not displayed.
/QT	Nothing is displayed during or after the install.
/QN1	Same as /Q1, except reboot is suppressed.
/QNT	Same as /QT, except reboot is suppressed.
/R	Forces a reinstall of the application. If this option is not used and the application has previously been installed, the user is prompted to add/remove, reinstall or remove all components.
/U	Uninstalls the application.
/UA	Uninstalls the application and removes shared components. These are components that are located outside of the application directory in shared locations such as the Visual FoxPro runtime or an ActiveX component.
/X filename	Creates (or appends to, if it exists) a text file that has one line for each install or uninstall that was done. Each line contains the following: the date, time, user, machine name, application name, application version and action (install or uninstall). The application administrator only needs to look at this file to see how many people have installed the application on the network. The file specified with the /G switch can be viewed if more detail is needed.
/Y	Copies the setup files into the application directory but does not install the application. The setup files are placed in a subdirectory called "setup."

The command line switches can be used together. For example, SETUP /QT /X superinvoice.txt does a silent install and logs the fact to a file.

With a Web executable, you have a different set of command line options. You can get a list of them by calling WebApp /?:

- /Q   Quiet modes for package
- /T: path   Specifies temporary working folder
- /C   Extracts files only to the folder when used also with /T
- /C: cmd   Overrides install command defined by author

The convenience of a single file and small size comes at a cost: the loss of control over the installation process.

Uninstalling the application

An application can be uninstalled by using the "Add/Remove Program" applet in the Control Panel or by using "SETUP /U." For a silent uninstall, use "SETUP.EXE /QT /U." (See MSKB Q173992 for more information.)

Configuring DCOM on client and server

DCOM is Distributed COM. Essentially it means that your COM components run on another computer. You might choose to implement DCOM to improve scalability and performance by spreading the work over several servers. The downside of DCOM is the overhead of calls across the network from the client to the server.

There is no need to install DCOM on Windows NT 4.0 or later because it is included. For Windows 95 or later, you can download DCOM and the configuration utility from these URLs:

- **www.microsoft.com/com/dcom/dcom95/download.asp**

- **www.microsoft.com/com/dcom/dcom98/download.asp**

DCOMCNFG.EXE (see **Figure 6**) is used to configure components on each of the Windows versions. It is located in the Windows system directory. On both the client and the server, you'll see four tabs:

- Applications—Provides a list of COM applications.

- Default Properties—Allows you to globally enable/disable DCOM, and set authentication and impersonation levels.

- Default Security—Allows you to set permissions for users to access, launch and configure DCOM components.

- Default Protocols—Allows you to select the protocol for DCOM communication. This tab is only available on Windows NT or later and Windows 2000, as Windows 95 or later only supports TCP/IP.

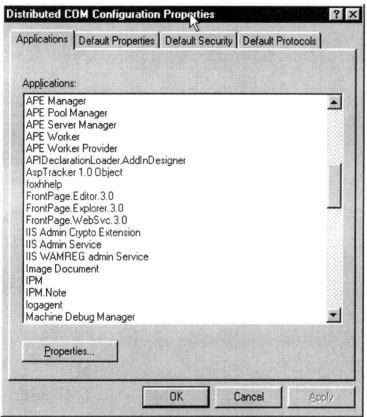

Figure 6*. The DCOMCNFG main screen on a computer with Windows 9x.*

On the Applications tab, choose a program, and then click Properties. You'll see a form (shown in **Figure 7**) with multiple tabs. On a client computer, they are:

- General—Specifies the application name, type, and path.

- Location—Specifies whether to run the application locally or specify a server.

- Security—Specifies whether to use the default permissions (specified in the main configuration dialog) or override it with user-specific permissions.

On a server computer, there are two more tabs:

- Identity—Specifies the user account under which to run the application.

- Endpoints—Allows custom values for protocols.

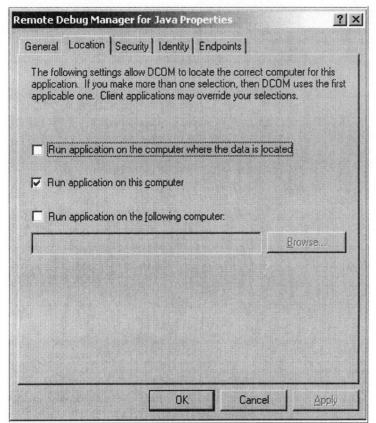

Figure 7. *The Location tab of a component on a client computer.*

Configuring a client to use an MTS component

First, you must create a package for the component on the server by running the Microsoft
Management Console (MMC) on the server. Start MMC by clicking Start, clicking Run, typing
mmc, and the pressing the Enter key. In the left pane, navigate down to Console Root | Microsoft
Transaction Server | Computers | My Computer | Packages Installed. Right-click and select
New | Package to start the Package Wizard. Click "Create an Empty Package" and enter the
name of the package. Choose which users can access this component. After you click the Finish
button, you will see the package in the right pane.

Now the package can be exported. Exporting a package means creating an installation
routine for the client computer to use the server component. Right-click on the package and
choose "Export," and then choose a location and name for the .PAK file. Once the export is
done, you will find a subfolder called "Clients" at the location you specified. This contains the
installation routine that you run on the client computer.

If you are having difficulty with Microsoft Management Console, an overview document is available at **www.microsoft.com/windows2000/library/howitworks/management/ mmcover.asp**.

Configure remote Automation on a client and server

Remote Automation is another method of accessing remote components. It was developed prior to DCOM. Most developers are familiar with Automation on a local computer. For example, you can use Automation from VFP to control Word or Excel. Remote Automation allows this type communication to happen between client and server computers.

Configuring a client and server for remote Automation is described in the last section of Chapter 16, "Adding OLE," in the *Microsoft Visual FoxPro 6.0 Programmer's Guide.*

Sample Questions

COM components are used in your application. How do you register them on a client computer?
   A. Include directions for your customers on how to use RegSvr32.
   B. Use a post-setup .EXE.
   C. Add the COM components to the install with the Setup Wizard's "Specify Components" screen.
   D. You can't, because COM components only run on servers.

Answer: C

How can you create a CD-based installation?
   A. Use the Netsetup option. If the installation is larger than 1 CD, use the Websetup option.
   B. You can't, but the next version of Visual FoxPro will support DVD.
   C. Use the floppy disk option and write a batch file to control the install.
   D. Use a third-party installation package.

Answer: A

Further reading

The Setup Wizard and installing an application

- *The Fundamentals: Building Visual Studio Applications on a Visual FoxPro 6.0 Foundation*, Whil Hentzen, Chapter 26, "Distributing Your Applications with the VFP Setup Wizard"

- *Microsoft Visual FoxPro 6.0 Programmer's Guide*, Chapter 13, "Compiling an Application"

- *Microsoft Visual FoxPro 6.0 Programmer's Guide*, Chapter 25, "Building an Application for Distribution"

- *Microsoft Visual FoxPro 6.0 Programmer's Guide*, Chapter 26, "Creating Distribution Disks"

- MSKB Q130664 "HOWTO: Use the Setup Wizard in Professional Visual FoxPro"

- MSKB Q194572 "HOWTO: Run an Unattended Setup of a Visual FoxPro Application"

- MSKB Q238553 "SAMPLE: VFPSCUT.EXE Creates Desktop Shortcut to a VFP Application"

- MSKB Q244677 "HOWTO: Create a Desktop Shortcut with the Windows Script Host"

Uninstalling an application

- MSKB Q173993 "HOWTO: Uninstall VFP Application Installed by Setup Wizard"

DCOM and MTS

- *Internet Applications with Visual FoxPro 6.0*, Rick Strahl, Chapter 5, "FoxISAPI"

- *MCSD VB6 Distributed Exam Cram*, Michael Lane Thomas and Dan Fox, Chapter 8, "Creating Business Services"

- *MCSD VB6 Distributed Exam Cram*, Michael Lane Thomas and Dan Fox, Chapter 11, "Distributing Applications"

- **http://msdn.microsoft.com/library/techart/mtsvfp.htm**

- **http://msdn.microsoft.com/library/backgrnd/html/msdn_dcomarch.htm**

- *Visual Basic 6 Distributed Exam Cram*, Chapter 11, "Distributing Applications"

- MSKB Q268550 "HOWTO: Use Dcomcnfg for a Visual Basic DCOM Client/Server Application"

- MSKB Q176799 "INFO: Using DCOM Config (DCOMCNFG.EXE) on Windows NT"

- MSKB Q182248 "HOWTO: Use DCOM Config (DCOMCNFG.EXE) with Windows 95/98"

- **www.west-wind.com/presentations/mts/mts.htm**

Remote Automation

- *Microsoft Visual FoxPro 6.0 Programmer's Guide*, Chapter 16, "Adding OLE"

Chapter 11
Maintaining and Supporting
an Application

You've finally gotten your application out the door. What happens next? If the users have been able to get your application working at all, they will soon start calling with lists of all those embarrassing bugs you didn't catch, and suggestions for improving the next version. Keeping track of all of this may require more than just a mental list or scraps of paper. Deploying updates may require different techniques than the initial install. Most of all, it's time to plan for the "big one" that could shut the users down and destroy all of their data.

If you supply custom software to a small organization, you may be the only software or hardware support they have, and it may be up to you to instruct them in all of the things they need to do to keep things running smoothly and safely. In other situations, you may be part of a team that ensures that the organization complies with government regulations before a government contract is awarded or an audit is done.

In the same way, handling errors for a small organization may just mean a verbal agreement to correct it soon, and for a larger application there may be the need to audit existing data to make sure the affected data is corrected or reprocessed.

Then there's the problem of actually making the updates. If the place shuts down daily at 5 PM, your job is easy. If your application supports a 24x7 operation such as a 911-call center, you may need more advance planning.

Let us tell you about one large IT shop Cindy worked for when she first learned FoxPro. When it was time to update the application, the programmers called the users in the building across the street and asked them all to log out of the application. There always seemed to be at least one computer left with the application open, and finding it was always a challenge. Meanwhile, 25 people were not working. It became quite a circus! Imagine how impressed Cindy was when she saw Alan Biddle demonstrate his award-winning 911-dispatch software and learned how nicely he handled application updates with very little interruption of service. What is a fairly common technique in the FoxPro world was a total eye-opener for Cindy at the time. She changed jobs shortly after that and immediately implemented Alan's techniques in the software she supported at her new job. Cindy also saw the danger of not having enough contact with other FoxPro developers—a problem that can result in remaining in the cave while the folks over the hill are building skyscrapers.

Planning and implementing disaster recovery procedures

Dr. Paul Rosenthal of California State University, Los Angeles, maintains that a Business Resumption Plan (BRP) is essential for protecting mission-critical operational and managerial functions in an organization. He suggests that two errors are common: thinking that chances of disaster are so slim that no planning is necessary, and thinking that the cost of planning exceeds the cost of the disaster if the disaster has a low possibility of occurring.

When making a BRP, the costs of implementing the plan should be balanced against the cost to the organization in lost business, not only from business missed during the recovery period, but from customers who are permanently lost because they went elsewhere during the recovery period. Obviously, a shorter recovery period will require that more funds be invested in the plan.

Disaster recovery plans need to include the accessibility of backup equipment, loading or upgrading software, restoring the data, and providing whatever hard-copy or other materials the users need to be up and running. Plans that include sharing local resources with another company work well for small disasters like a fire in an individual building, but they won't be of much help when a disaster strikes everyone in town. In that case, plans need to be made for use of a facility outside of the disaster area and the availability of personnel to man the facility.

Most of you won't be doing anything on this scale without a lot of input from people who specialize in this sort of thing, so let's talk about situations you could easily find yourself in.

- The user thinks the machine is "locked up" and pulls the plug, destroying the table headers.

- The roof leaks on the server and the hard drive crashes, destroying all of the data since the last backup.

- A little mess requires a restore, but the backup mechanism hasn't worked for the past two months, and nobody bothered reading the logs to notice.

- Backups have carefully and faithfully been made on the same 10 tapes for so long that the tapes are no longer usable for a restore.

- The "big one" occurs.

We've all encountered these very situations often enough to know that the probability is high that they will happen, and we definitely want to plan for them. We can't control when they will happen, but we can minimize their impact.

Table corruption

Table header corruption is a definite possibility in FoxPro. So definite that it's worth learning how to do table repairs. If your users are not onsite, it's worth purchasing third-party table header repair software and including it with your applications. Some software can detect and repair table header problems automatically, or you may need to write some wrapper code or supply the software separately with instructions on how to use it. There is also third-party software available that corrects problems in the data or memo fields. We've included a list of third-party software at the end of this chapter. One good thing to do before attempting to repair a memo file is to MODIFY FILE MyDbf.FPT, which brings the memo file up in a text editor. If the data looks coherent, it's worth saving. If not, you need to use the backup.

You can maintain indexes by regularly using DELETE TAG ALL and rebuilding them. Unfortunately, deleting index tags that are involved in persistent relationships will break the relationships. However, if you run GenDBC.PRG on your database, you can copy the pieces of code that generate the relations and re-run them. In fact, it's always a good idea to run GenDBC on your database.

There is also a third-party software package, Stonefield Database Toolkit, to do data dictionary chores automatically, including rebuilding views when table definitions change and rebuilding indexes. Table maintenance can be scheduled to run when the users are out of the system, or to begin when the first user logs in. Other users get a "please wait" message and know that the system will be available by the time they get their coffee cups filled and are back at their desks.

Restoring data since the last backup

In the usual scenario, a problem stops work in mid-day and a table is wiped out. The overnight backup is successfully restored. The application supports hundreds of transactions per hour, and data entered since the last backup appears to be lost. This situation would definitely be a problem for a mission-critical application!

You can be prepared for problems like this by incorporating transaction logging into your applications. Write your own, or consider purchasing FoxAudit from **www.takenote.com**. Calls to FoxAudit can easily be put in FoxPro's insert, update, and delete triggers in the .DBC, and FoxAudit's roll forward/roll back capabilities make it easy to roll the data forward from the overnight backup to the time of the event.

An important consideration here is that the whole database should be restored to be current with the individual table that was damaged or missing.

Backups that don't work

A good Business Resumption Plan should include prevention and "fire drills." That means that not only should you make arrangements for the data to be backed up at appropriate intervals, you should also test the backup procedure to make sure that the data is in fact being copied, and that the data can be restored from the copy. This includes not only the initial testing, but also "auditing" the procedure at regular intervals. Backup logs should be read for anomalies. Test restores should be performed. Tapes or other backup media should be rotated, including storing backups offsite. The backup media should be checked for signs of aging. At one job, Cindy was instructed to take the backup tape home with her if she could not get it safely stored in the bank vault overnight! If the organization is large enough or the application and data mission-critical, periodic backups should also be sent to a location that is more than a few miles away from the main data store.

FoxPro has the ability to copy files that are open. This means that a "roll your own" backup procedure can run even if someone has gone home and left a table open. Supplementing the automatic nightly backup with a copy routine run occasionally within your application might be useful.

The "big one"

You just never know when a large disaster will wipe out everyone in town. In fact, Microsoft's Redmond campus is experiencing the aftermath of an earthquake as we prepare this chapter for publication!

Arrangements to use your neighbor's network at night, while a suitable BRP for the event of a fire or server meltdown, won't work if you and your neighbor are both in the same disastrous state. Of course, you won't lose customers to the competing small business on the next block during this time if you, the competition and your customer base are all busy cutting down fallen trees or drying out your basements, but a larger operation should definitely have a suitable BRP including an out-of-state computer installation and personnel to man it.

Correcting errors and preventing future errors

Now we'll move on to a topic that's a little closer to home: program bugs. Fortunately, programming errors are a little easier to prevent or control than the disasters mentioned earlier, but unfortunately they are usually our fault! We discuss techniques for testing and debugging in Chapter 9, "Testing and Debugging the Solution," and hopefully, your error trapping routine has provided you with sufficient information to begin identifying the source of the error. Once you've found the bug, you'll want to take the necessary steps to correct it and then reevaluate the data in light of the changes. While you've got the users out of the system, you'll want to do a little maintenance and see whether anything else needs improvement or refactoring since you passed through this code the last time. (Cindy's code is full of notes to herself about things to review or refactor!) We will discuss each of the following issues:

- The joys of object-oriented bug fixes

- Reevaluating the data

- Table maintenance

- View maintenance

- Using a local .DBC for views

The joys of object-oriented bug fixes

In these days of object-oriented programming, bug fixing is simplified by the nature of object orientation. We only have to change the code in one place for our changes to be inherited throughout all of our applications that use that particular code. What happens after that is important, however. Does the bug fix "break" any other code? This type of testing, called Regression Testing, is discussed further in Chapter 9, "Testing and Debugging the Solution."

Reevaluating the data

Whenever an error that affects data integrity is corrected, all of the data should be reevaluated in light of the change. Referential integrity rules within the .DBC will take care of orphan prevention, and a good normalized database design will make changes to data quick and easy. If the database has been denormalized, you need to take special care to check all of the places where the data might be affected.

Many problems can be prevented through proper maintenance of the tables. A first defense is to run GenDBC.PRG on your database after every change. The resulting program (MyData.PRG, for example) is useful to rebuild all of the tables and views, their indexes, stored procedures, referential integrity constraints and connections. Individual pieces of this code can be vitally important, as we will see in a moment.

Table maintenance

Packing tables can be done as part of the regular table maintenance routine, assuming that the user would like deleted records to be completely removed. In large tables with a lot of deletions, record recycling routines are often used as a method to eliminate the need for packing the tables, and the downtime associated with it.

Indexes should be completely dropped (DELETE TAG ALL) and recreated wherever possible. The reason for this is that any corruption within an index tag is perpetuated by the REINDEX command. In addition, rebuilding the indexes reduces index bloat. The problem with DELETE TAG ALL is that any persistent relationships or referential integrity constraints that are dependent on these indexes are "broken" when the indexes are dropped. This is where the program created by GenDBC helps out. You can paste the code from MyData.PRG into your housekeeping routine and easily recreate the indexes, persistent relationships, and referential integrity constraints that way. Third-party software can do this chore for you also. (See the "Table corruption" section earlier in this chapter.)

View maintenance

Views are sometimes "broken" when the underlying table structure changes. A broken view cannot be opened in the View Designer for repairs. This can easily result in having to step through the View Designer numerous times in the course of getting an application running and out the door. The View Designer also has some limits on the number and type of joins it can handle.

The best approach for creating views is to begin defining the view in the View Designer, and then view the SQL or run GenDBC, and copy the code to a .PRG file. This method saves you from having to type (and possibly misspell) all of the table and field names, and GenDBC will capture all of the appropriate settings. You can then further edit the program to finish the joins and whatever other fine-tuning the view needs. Then be sure to run GenDBC again to capture the view in its final state, and again, copy the code to the .PRG file. After that, fixing a broken view is as simple as adding or deleting a few lines of SQL code or changing a few properties.

The VFP View Designer is somewhat limited, but Erik Moore's eView utility picks up where it leaves off. Once you've written the SQL statement for the view, fire up eView to set the view properties visually and generate a program to create the view. You can find more details on eView later in this chapter.

Using a local .DBC for views

When a user requeries a view, VFP locks the .DBC record containing the view information. Until the query results are returned, no one else can requery their view, whether they are trying to access the same data records or not. This is not noticeable with a small number of users, but it can become a problem as more users are added to the system.

The solution is to have a view-only .DBC residing on the user's hard drive. It can be updated whenever necessary with the loader described later in this chapter. Changes in database design can take care of the problems associated with having the correct database current when the views and tables are opened.

Keeping track of problems

Keeping track of the status of errors and updates to correct them can be as simple as a scribbled note, or as complex as a full application just for this purpose. Some data analysis contracts require that the version number of the application be noted with each data point and that the data be reevaluated after a bug fix to see whether its status will change. All of these can make bug tracking and version changes a more involved process.

Microsoft has made ATSWeb, an anomaly tracking system written in Visual FoxPro, available as a free download from **http://msdn.microsoft.com/vfoxpro/downloads/ ats_download.asp**.

User reporting of errors can also be simple or complex. Obviously, if you're not in proximity to the users, they can't call you and ask you to come see their computer screen! To have the results of AERROR() and the current memory variables logged to a file, use a combination of FoxPro commands. SAVE TO will save the current values to a memo field or .MEM file, which can be used to restore all of the values back to memory (RESTORE FROM) should you find it useful in your debugging. Use LIST STATUS and LIST MEMORY (see DISPLAY in Help) for text representations of the memory variables. There are even routines available to make a screen shot to include in the bug report! You can have the error routine send e-mail to the helpdesk, dial your pager, and so forth. Of course, you'll want to filter the errors that call your pager!

Deploying application updates

Distributing your application for the first time is covered in detail in Chapter 10, "Deploying an Application." At some point you will want to distribute updates to your application. Perhaps there is a service pack because the users have asked for additional features. We would all like to pretend that *our* applications *never* need bug fixes, but we might as well admit that it happens!

Deploying updates brings us to a few issues that aren't present with the initial deployment. They include:

- Making changes to an existing database

- Minimizing update size and simplifying deployment

- Updating the application while minimizing user downtime

Making changes to an existing database

At times you will need to add or change table fields when you deploy an update to an application. This is best done programmatically with ALTER TABLE commands, and it will need to be done at a time when there can be exclusive use of the tables. You can also purchase third-party software, listed at the end of this chapter, which will do this for you.

As mentioned earlier, special care must be taken with persistent relationships and referential integrity constraints when changing table structures. They can be rebuilt with the code produced by GenDBC.

Minimizing update size and simplifying deployment

Updates to your application can be welcomed by the users or represent an annoyance, depending in part on how easy they are to apply. Deploying the updates once on a network drive is certainly easier than updating each workstation individually, and we'll discuss ways to accomplish that in a moment.

Hopefully, you have created a subdirectory on the network or shared drive and put into it everything needed to install your application the first time. This is where any updates to the application should be copied.

The updates themselves can be distributed via diskettes, CDs, e-mail, or FTP. Depending on your situation, you can copy them into the subdirectory yourself or appoint a power user at each installation to do these chores. You may have easy access to the network where this subdirectory resides, or be separated by thousands of miles and a firewall. Your power user may be well-educated and computer-literate, or barely know how to navigate a keyboard, and this will determine how far you have to go in making the updates simple to perform.

To avoid having to distribute a large file each time one small change is made, the application can be broken into smaller sections that are called from the main application. The multi-tier architecture model lends itself well to separately distributable pieces. Graphic files can be excluded from the project and distributed separately, as can reports.

Updating the application while minimizing user downtime

When Cindy watched Alan Biddle's demonstration of his software, she saw her first "loader" application. Loaders come in a lot of different flavors, and some examples can be found on the Universal Thread, but here are the principles that drive them:

- The loader application is installed once and seldom changes. It will need to be installed on each client machine, but the installation will not need to be repeated every time a change is made to the main application.

- The loader application has some way of knowing when a new update has been copied into the network or shared directory. In Alan's case, the name and version number of the new file were stored in a small text file on the network. The name of the new executable was edited into the text file when the updates were made. This allowed several older versions to be kept online. Other loaders compare the timestamp on the new executable in the network subdirectory to the one that resides on the client machine. If this type of loader is in use, there needs to be a way to revert to a previous version of the executable if there is a problem.

- The shortcut on the user's desktop points to the loader, not the application itself.

- Each time the loader is run, it checks the application subdirectory on the network to see whether there is anything new. If there are any new files, it copies them to the local drive and does any other installation chores. The loader can then call the main application or start the main application in another process and quit itself.

- Whenever a new version is made available on the network, all the user needs to do to have the new version load on his hard drive is close out of the application and start it again. A messaging system, run by a timer, could check the update directory for new updates and notify the user when one was made available. The user could be notified to log out as soon as possible or at his convenience.

- Table structure changes, or anything else that requires exclusive use of the tables, need to be done when the users are totally out of the system, or when the first user logs in for the day.

Sample Question

Your customer's business has grown rapidly, and the original five users have just trained 20 additional staff. They are mystified by the fact that the search forms have become very sluggish when retrieving data. You know that the search forms use parameterized views. Which of the following actions is most likely to improve the situation with the least amount of redesign of the application?
A. Upsize the data to Microsoft SQL Server, because FoxPro tables are slow with more than five users.
B. Lock the view definition in the .DBC each time it is requeried so no other user can change it.
C. Move all of the views to a separate .DBC on the server so there won't be any contention issues between the tables and the views in the .DBC.
D. Move all of the views to a separate .DBC on the client so there won't be any contention issues between the users for the view definition in the .DBC.

Answer: D

Further reading

- "BUSINESS RESUMPTION PLANNING: Justification, Implementation & Testing," Dr. Paul Rosenthal, **www.bizforum.org/whitepapers/calstatela.htm**

- **http://fox.wikis.com/wc.dll?Wiki~DisasterRecoveryProcedures**

- The Rothstein Associates, Inc. Web site at **www.rothstein.com**: Rothstein Associates provides consulting services to companies in need of disaster recovery planning. The Web site features a series of original articles and a good list of books on the subject.

Third-party software

Anomaly tracking

- ATSWeb, an anomaly tracking system written in Visual FoxPro and available from Microsoft, **http://msdn.microsoft.com/vfoxpro/downloads/ats_download**

Database maintenance

- eView by Erik Moore, #971, Visual FoxPro Downloads, **www.universalthread.com**, Public domain, .EXE without source code

- Stonefield Systems Group: Stonefield Database Toolkit provides full data dictionary support including changing table structures, rebuilding views and adding or rebuilding indexes. **www.stonefield.com**

Loaders

- AppLauncher by Fred Lauckner, #1144, Visual FoxPro Downloads, **www.universalthread.com**, Public domain, .EXE without source code

- Launcher by Nick Neklioudov, #1186, Visual FoxPro Downloads, **www.universalthread.com**, Public domain, source code included

- MkStart by Milan Kosina, #1335, Visual FoxPro Downloads, **www.universalthread.com**, Public domain, .EXE without source code

- SysLaunch by Kenneth Downs, #1090, Visual FoxPro Downloads, **www.universalthread.com**, Public domain, source code included

Screen shots

- Print Screens From VFP (ScrnPrnt) by Steve Ruhl, #966, Visual FoxPro Downloads, **www.universalthread.com**, Public domain, source code included, royalty-free redistribution subject to Microsoft license of the WinCap32 code

- TechSmith: SnagIt: A powerful screen capture utility to capture images, text and video from your Windows desktop. **www.techsmith.com**

Table repair

- Abri Technologies: Recover, a comprehensive, automatic, FoxPro file error detection and recovery utility. Automatic detection and salvage/repair of table headers, table records and memo files. **www.abri.com**

- HexEdit: found in \Tools\Hexedit in your VFP home directory. Directions for repairing tables can be found at **http://fox.wikis.com/wc.dll?Wiki~NotATable**.

- Stonefield Systems Group: Stonefield Database Toolkit, repairs corrupted table and memo headers. **www.stonefield.com**

- Xitech: FoxFix, an intuitive GUI tool for analyzing, examining and repairing table corruption and a library that can be distributed with an application to automatically detect and repair tables. **www.foxfix.com**

Transaction logging

- TakeNote Technologies: FoxAudit, add complete, automatic, client/server-like audit trail support to the Visual FoxPro database container. **www.takenote.com**

- Red Matrix Technologies: SQLAudit, add audit trail support to SQL Server 7 databases. **www.redmatrix.com**

Index